Donna Kooler's 555 Cross-Stitch Motifs

Sterling Publishing Co., Inc. New York
A Sterling/Chapelle Book

Chapelle Ltd.

Owner: Jo Packham

Editor: Karmen Quinney

Graphic Coordinator: Susan Jorgensen

Staff: Areta Bingham, Kass Burchett,
Jill Dahlberg, Marilyn Goff, Holly Hollingsworth,
Barbara Milburn, Linda Orton, Cindy Stoeckl,
Kim Taylor, Sara Toliver, Desirée Wybrow

Photography: Kevin Dilley/Hazen Photo Studio

Kooler Design Studio, Inc.

President: Donna Kooler

Vice President & Editor: Priscilla Timm

Executive Vice President: Linda Gillum

Staff Designers: Barbara Baatz, Linda Gillum,
Nancy Rossi, Jorja Hernandez, Sandy Orton,
Thomas Taneyhill, Pam Johnson

Design Assistants: Sara Angle, Jennifer Drake,
Laurie Grant, Virginia Hanley-Rivett,
Marsha Hinkson, Karen Million, Char Randolph,
Connie Regner

Library of Congress Cataloging-in-Publication Data

Kooler, Donna.
  Donna Kooler's 555 Cross-stitch motifs.
     p. cm.
  Includes index.
  ISBN 0-8069-3758-0
  1. Cross-stitch—Patterns. I. Title: 555 cross-stitch motifs. II. Title.

TT778.C76 K6662 2002
746.44'3041—dc21   2001049751

10 9 8 7 6 5 4 3 2 1

Published by Sterling Publishing Company, Inc.,
387 Park Avenue South, New York, NY 10016
© 2002 by Kooler Design Studio, Inc.
Distributed in Canada by Sterling Publishing
⅓ Canadian Manda Group, One Atlantic Avenue, Suite 105
Toronto, Ontario, Canada M6K 3E7
Distributed in Great Britain and Europe by Cassell PLC
Wellington House, 125 Strand, London WC2R 0BB, England
Distributed in Australia by Capricorn Link (Australia) Pty. Ltd.
P.O. Box 704, Windsor, NSW 2756, Australia
Printed in USA
All Rights Reserved

Sterling ISBN 0-8069-3758-0

If you have any questions or comments, please contact: Chapelle, Ltd., Inc., P.O. Box 9252 Ogden, UT 84409 (801) 621-2777 • FAX (801) 621-2788 e-mail: chapelle@ chapelleltd.com website: www.chapelleltd.com

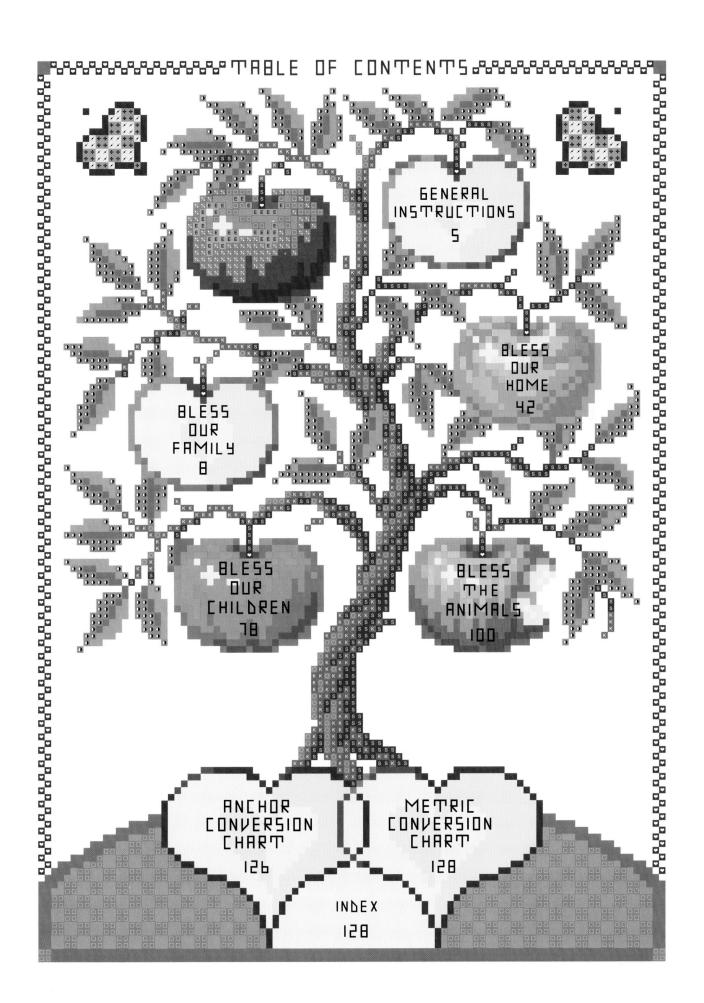

TABLE OF CONTENTS

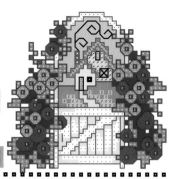

Home Sweet Home

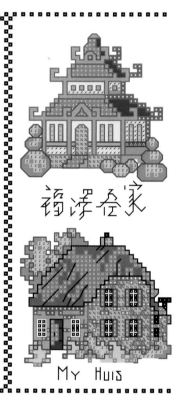

福泽吾家

*May peace
and plenty
bless your world,
with joy that
long endures.*

Mi Casa

My Huis

WELCOME TO OUR HOME AWAY FROM HOME

LOVE MAKES A HOUSE a HOME

A WOMAN'S HOME IS HER CASTLE

General Instructions

Introduction

Contained in this book are over 555 cross-stitch designs. Each double-page spread of graphed designs has its own color code. Each sampler's code is placed with the graphed sampler. To create one-of-a-kind motifs, vary colors in graphed designs.

For backstitching, use one strand on all fabrics. When completing a French Knot (FK), use one strand and one wrap on all fabrics, unless otherwise directed.

Cross-stitch Items to Know

Fabric for Cross-stitch

Counted cross-stitch is worked on even-weave fabrics. These fabrics are manufactured specifically for counted-thread embroidery, and are woven with the same number of vertical as horizontal threads per inch.

Because the number of threads in the fabric is equal in each direction, each stitch will be the same size. The number of threads per inch in even-weave fabrics determines the size of a finished design.

Number of Strands

The number of strands used per stitch varies, depending on the fabric used. Generally, the rule to follow for cross-stitching is three strands on Aida 11, two strands on Aida 14, one or two strands on Aida 18 (depending on desired thickness of stitches), and one strand on Hardanger 22.

Finished Design Size

To determine the size of the finished design, divide the stitch count by the number of threads per inch of fabric. When a design is stitched over two threads, divide stitch count by half the threads per inch. For example, if a design with a stitch count of 120 width and 250 height was stitched on a 28 count linen (over two threads making it 14 count), the finished size would be 8⅝" x 17⅞".

$$120 \div 14" = 8\tfrac{5}{8}" \ (width)$$

$$250 \div 14" = 17\tfrac{7}{8}" \ (height)$$

$$Finished\ size = 8\tfrac{5}{8}" \times 17\tfrac{7}{8}"$$

Preparing Fabric

Cut fabric at least 3" larger on all sides than the finished design size to ensure enough space for desired assembly. To prevent fraying, whipstitch or machine-zigzag along the raw edges or apply liquid fray preventive.

Needles for Cross-stitch

Blunt needles should slip easily through the fabric holes without piercing fabric threads. For fabric with 11 or fewer threads per inch, use a tapestry needle #24; for 14 threads per inch, use a tapestry needle #24, #26, or #28; for 18 or more threads per inch, use a tapestry needle #26 or #28. Avoid leaving the needle in the design area of the fabric. It may leave rust or a permanent impression on the fabric.

Floss

All numbers and color names on the codes represent the DMC brand of floss. Use 18" lengths of floss. For best coverage, separate the strands and dampen with a wet sponge, then put together the number of strands required for the fabric used.

Page 125

Centering Design on Fabric

Fold the fabric in half horizontally, then vertically. Place a pin in the intersection to mark the center. Locate the center of the design on the graph. To help in centering the designs, dots are provided at the center top or bottom and center side. Begin stitching all designs at the center point of the graph and fabric. Black outlines extending from graphs indicate repeat of design.

Securing Floss

Insert needle up from the underside of the fabric at starting point. Hold 1" of thread behind the fabric and stitch over it, securing with the first few stitches. To finish thread, run under four or more stitches on the back of the design. Avoid knotting floss, unless working on clothing.

Another method of securing floss is the waste knot. Knot floss and insert needle down from the right top side of the fabric about 1" from design area. Work several stitches over the thread to secure. Cut off the knot later.

Carrying Floss

To carry floss, run floss under the previously worked stitches on the back. Do not carry thread across any fabric that is not or will not be stitched. Loose threads, especially dark ones, will show through the fabric.

Cleaning Finished Design

When stitching is finished, soak the fabric in cold water with a mild soap for five to ten minutes. Rinse well and roll in a towel to remove excess water. Do not wring. Place the piece face down on a dry towel and iron on a warm setting until the fabric is dry.

Page 89

Stitching Techniques

Backstitch (BS)

1. Insert needle up between woven threads at A.

2. Go down at B, one opening to the right.

3. Come up at C.

4. Go down at A, one opening to the right.

Page 98

Cross-stitch (XS)

Stitches are done in a row or, if necessary, one at a time in an area.

1. Insert needle up between woven threads at A.

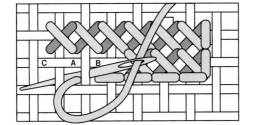

2. Go down at B, the opening diagonally across from A.

3. Come up at C and go down at D, etc.

4. To complete the top stitches creating an "X", come up at E and go down at B, come up at C and go down at F, etc. All top stitches should lie in the same direction.

French Knot (FK)

1. Insert needle up between woven threads at A, using one strand of embroidery floss.

2. Loosely wrap floss once around needle.

3. Go down at B, the opening across from A. Pull floss taut as needle is pushed down through fabric.

4. Carry floss across back of work between knots.

Long Stitch (LS)

1. Insert needle up between woven threads at A.

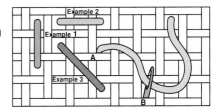

2. Go down at B, crossing two threads. Pull flat.

3. Repeat Steps 1–2 for each stitch. Stitch may be horizontal, vertical, or diagonal as indicated in Examples 1, 2, and 3. The length of the stitch should be the same as the length indicated on the graph.

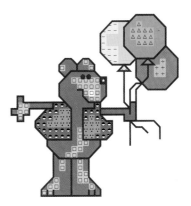

Page 26

Bless
Our
Family

Bless Our Family Sampler

DMC Floss	XS	BS	FK
White	·		
746	▫		
677	✎		
676	▪		○
729	✚		
3828	◉		
3829	▪		
*202HL	Z		
945	▫		
722	E		
721	▪		
920	★		
350	▨		
347	▪	⌐	
814	▪	⌐	
3689	▫		
3688	+		
3687	△		
3803	H	⌐	●
340	▪		
3746	◘		
333	✳	⌐	●
3840	▫		
3839	▣		○
3838	N	⌐	
472 / 471	▪		
989	▣		
987	▪	⌐	
986	M		
503	▪		
502	◑		
501	▪	⌐	
434	K	⌐	
898	S		●
*202HL / 898		⌐	
3371	♥	⌐	
453	▫		
647	▪		
646	▲		
535	▪		●

*Kreinik blending filament

10

Bless Our Family Sampler   Top Left

DMC Floss

	XS	BS	FK
White	·		
746			
677			
676			○
729	✚		
3828	◌		
3829			
*202HL	Z		
945			
722	E		
721			
920	★		
350			
347	■	⌐	
814	■	⌐	
3689			
3688	+		
3687	△		
3803	H	⌐	●
340			
3746	▫		
333	✳	⌐	●
3840			
3839	⁛		●
3838	N	⌐	
472 471 }			
989			
987		⌐	
986	M		
503			
502	◑		
501		⌐	
434	K	⌐	
898	S		●
*202HL 898 }		⌐	
3371	♥	⌐	
453			
647	⊞		
646	▲		
535	■		●
*Kreinik blending filament			

13

fall far from
the tree

ILY IS A CIRCLE OF CARING AND SHARING

XANDRA
MPTON
25 · 55

MICHAEL
ANDERSON
10 · 30 · 53

MARRIED
APRIL 30 1980

DMC Floss			
	XS	**BS**	**FK**
White	·		
746	☐		
677	◪		
676	▦		●
729	✚		
3828	◉		
3829	■		
*202HL	Z		
945	▦		
722	E		
721	■		
920	★		
350	▨		
347	■	⌐	
814	■	⌐	
3689	☐		
3688	⊞		
3687	◬		
3803	H	⌐	●
340	■		
3746	▣		
333	✳	⌐	●
3840	▦		
3839	⊡		●
3838	N	⌐	
472 } 471	▨		
989	▣		
987	■	⌐	
986	M		
503	▨		
502	◐		
501	■	⌐	
434	K	⌐	
898	S		●
*202HL } 898		⌐	
3371	♥	⌐	
453	▦		
647	▣		
646	◮		
535	■		●
*Kreinik blending filament			

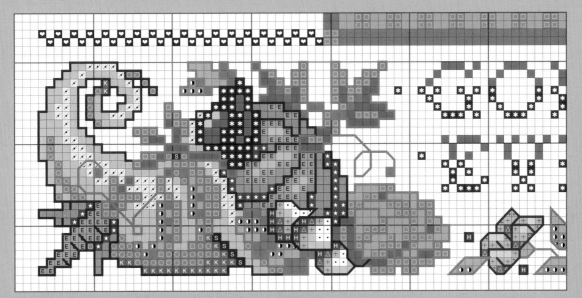

Bottom Left

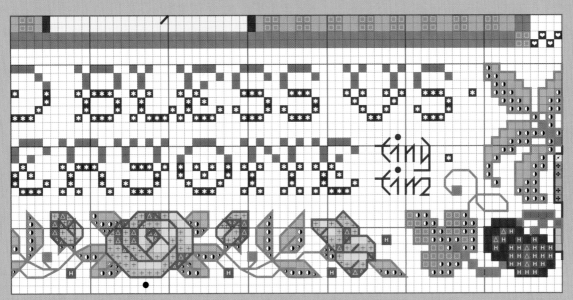

Bottom Center

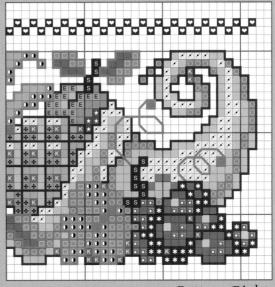

Bottom Right

DMC Floss			
	XS	BS	FK
White	·		
677	▫		
744	+		
3855	▨		
741	▪		
740		⌐	
948	▫		
963	▬		
776	U		
899	▪		
3350		⌐	●
3609	⊡		
3607	▪	⌐	
211	▫		
209	H		
554	▪		
327		⌐	
3761	▫		
3840	△		
800	S		
3325	▨		
809		⌐	
813	▪		
825		⌐	
932		⌐	
312	■	⌐	
3811	◈		
597	+		
772	▫		
913	◉		
912	▪		
3809		⌐	
3364	▨		
3363	▨		
319		⌐	
3773	▪		
3772		⌐	
437	E		
976		⌐	
3826	▨		
434	▪	⌐	
415	▪		
318	▨	⌐	
413	■	⌐	●

DMC Floss			
	XS	**BS**	**FK**
White	·		
3823			
677			
676			
745	–		
744	Z		
3855	U		
3854			
783		⌐	
3706			
3801	+		
321			
818	×		
963			
962	△		
3354			
335			
3689	+		
3688	○		
3609	M		
326	E	⌐	●
815	✛	⌐	
3743			
211	◇		
333	■	⌐	
828	J		
3761	S		
3756			
3755		⌐	
800	□		
3840	K		
3325			
794	H		
813			
340			
825		⌐	
932	N	⌐	
931		⌐	
369			
368			
955	G		
913			
911		⌐	
3348	▽		
3347			
986	★	⌐	●
435		⌐	
433		⌐	●
762			
414		⌐	
317		⌐	●

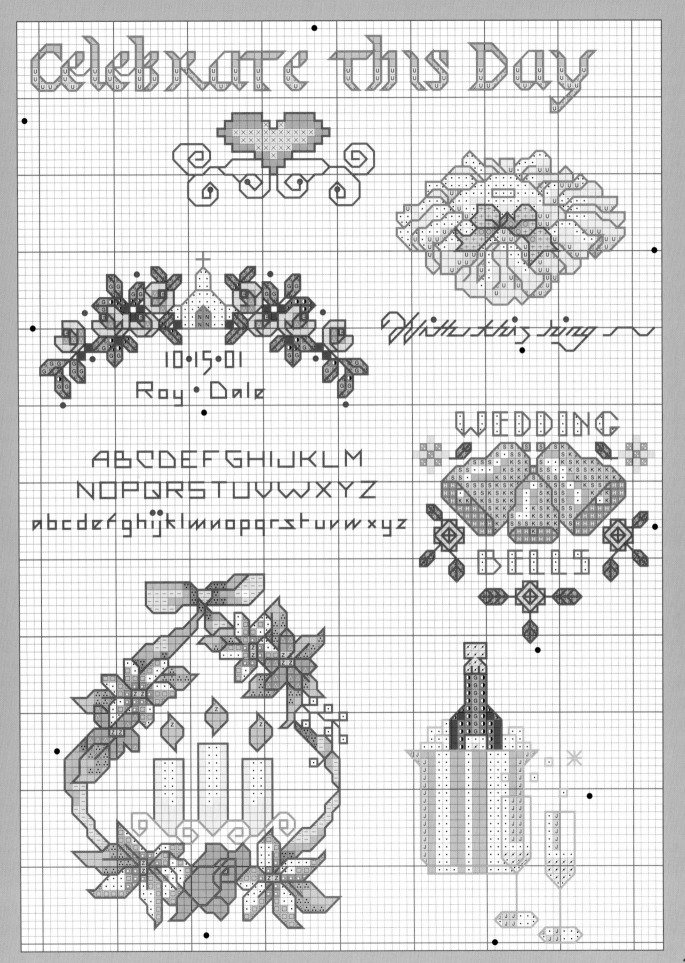

Celebrate this Day

10·15·01
Roy • Dale

With this ring...

WEDDING

BELLS

ABCDEFGHIJKLM
NOPQRSTUVWXYZ
abcdefghijklmnopqrstuvwxyz

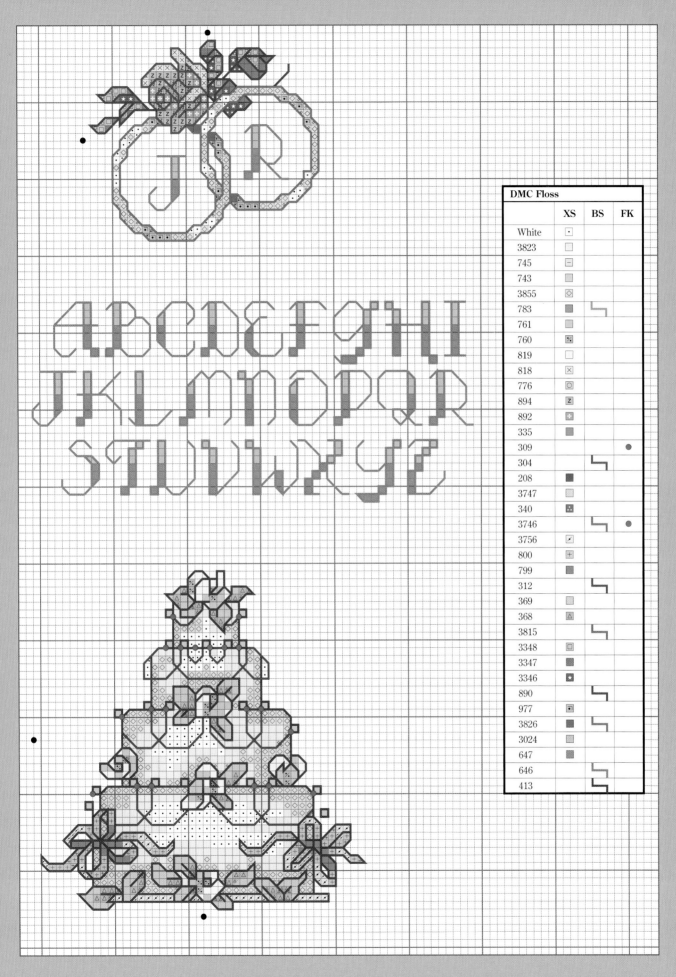

DMC Floss			
	XS	BS	FK
White	·		
3823			
745	−		
743			
3855	◇		
783	■	⌐	
761			
760	▨		
819			
818	✕		
776	◎		
894	z		
892	✛		
335	■		
309			●
304		⌐	
208	■		
3747			
340	▨		
3746		⌐	●
3756	◪		
800	+		
799	■		
312		⌐	
369			
368	△		
3815		⌐	
3348	▢		
3347	▨		
3346	★		
890		⌐	
977	▣		
3826	■	⌐	
3024			
647	▨		
646		⌐	
413		⌐	

GROOM

BRIDE

Bless this Union

To My Love

DMC Floss			
	XS	**BS**	**FK**
White	·		
745	−		
743	∴		
3855	✗		
3853		⌐	
676	▣		
783	▨		
818	⊠		
963	+		
776	U		
899	N		
957	◮		
3716	E		
335		⌐	●
3731	H		
3689	▢		
3688	▨		
3354	▣		
3350	▦		
3609	◎		
3608	✦		
3607	■		
3803	★	⌐	
351	▨		
349	▨		
3705	S		
666	▽		
321	❋		
815	♥	⌐	
211	▢		
209	▨		
3837		⌐	●
3761	▢		
800	Z		
813	▨		
825		⌐	
368	▢		
319	■	⌐	
563	▨		
3815	◨		
472			
3013	K		
3012	▨		
3348	◇		
3347	▼		
977	W	⌐	
3826	▨	⌐	
415	▨		
317	■		
413		⌐	●

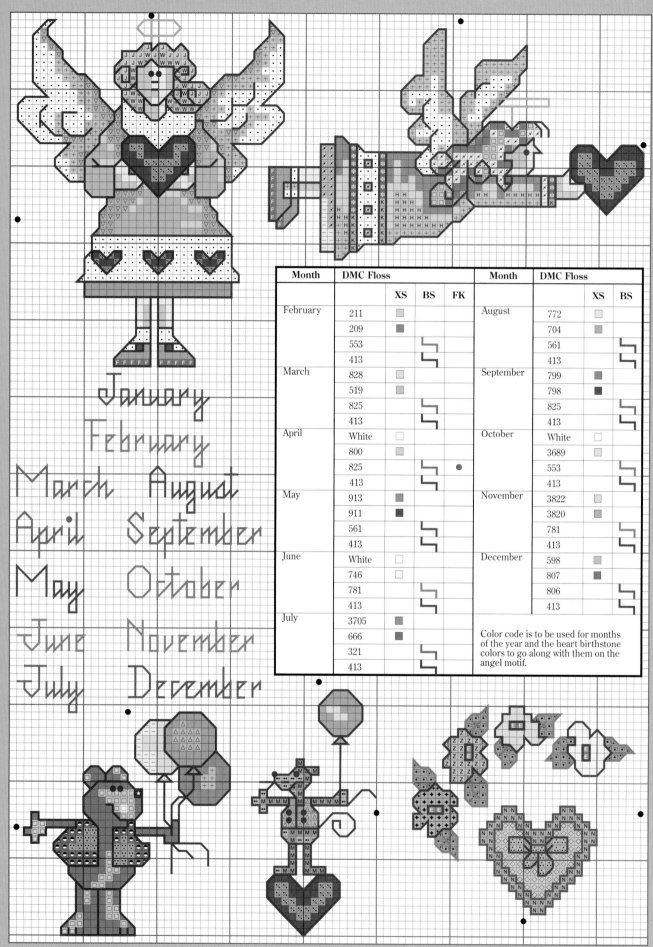

January

February

March   August

April   September

May   October

June   November

July   December

Month	DMC Floss	XS	BS	FK	Month	DMC Floss	XS	BS
February	211	▨			August	772	▨	
	209	▨				704	▨	
	553		⌐			561		⌐
	413		⌐			413		⌐
March	828	▨			September	799	▨	
	519	▨				798	▨	
	825		⌐			825		⌐
	413		⌐			413		⌐
April	White	☐			October	White	☐	
	800	▨				3689	▨	
	825		⌐	●		553		⌐
	413		⌐			413		⌐
May	913	▨			November	3822	▨	
	911	▨				3820	▨	
	561		⌐			781		⌐
	413		⌐			413		⌐
June	White	☐			December	598	▨	
	746	☐				807	▨	
	781		⌐			806		⌐
	413		⌐			413		⌐
July	3705	▨						
	666	▨						
	321		⌐					
	413		⌐					

Color code is to be used for months of the year and the heart birthstone colors to go along with them on the angel motif.

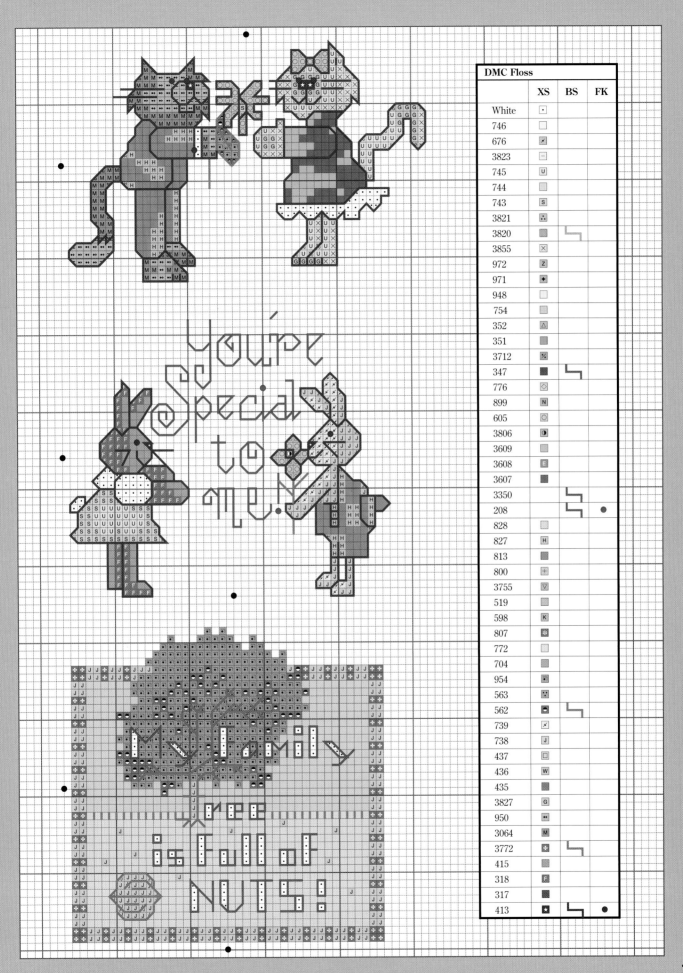

DMC Floss			
	XS	BS	FK
White	·		
746	□		
676	◪		
3823	⊟		
745	U		
744	▢		
743	S		
3821	⊡		
3820	▨	⌐	
3855	⊠		
972	Z		
971	✦		
948	□		
754	▢		
352	△		
351	▨		
3712	▨		
347	▨	⌐	
776	◇		
899	N		
605	○		
3806	◑		
3609	▨		
3608	E		
3607	▨		
3350		⌐	
208		⌐	●
828	▢		
827	H		
813	▨		
800	⊞		
3755	⋁		
519	▨		
598	K		
807	▨		
772	▢		
704	▨		
954	▪		
563	⊡		
562	▣	⌐	
739	◪		
738	J		
437	▢		
436	W		
435	▨		
3827	G		
950	⟩⟩		
3064	M		
3772	▨	⌐	
415	▨		
318	F		
317	▨		
413	▨	⌐	●

DMC Floss			
	XS	BS	FK
White	·		
3823			
745	–		
744			
743			
742	△		
741		⌐	
729			
3825			
3340		⌐	
948			
818	⊘		
776			
899	E		
335			
605	+		
309		⌐	●
3609	·		
3607			
718		⌐	
211			
210			
209	+		
554	H		
552		⌐	●
3756	×		
800			
3325			
334		⌐	
799			
3761	U		
3348			
3347			
772	○		
955			
954	N		
562		⌐	
911			
704	▽		
703	+		
702	K		
701			
699		⌐	●
402	Z	⌐	
301		⌐	
318		⌐	
413		⌐	

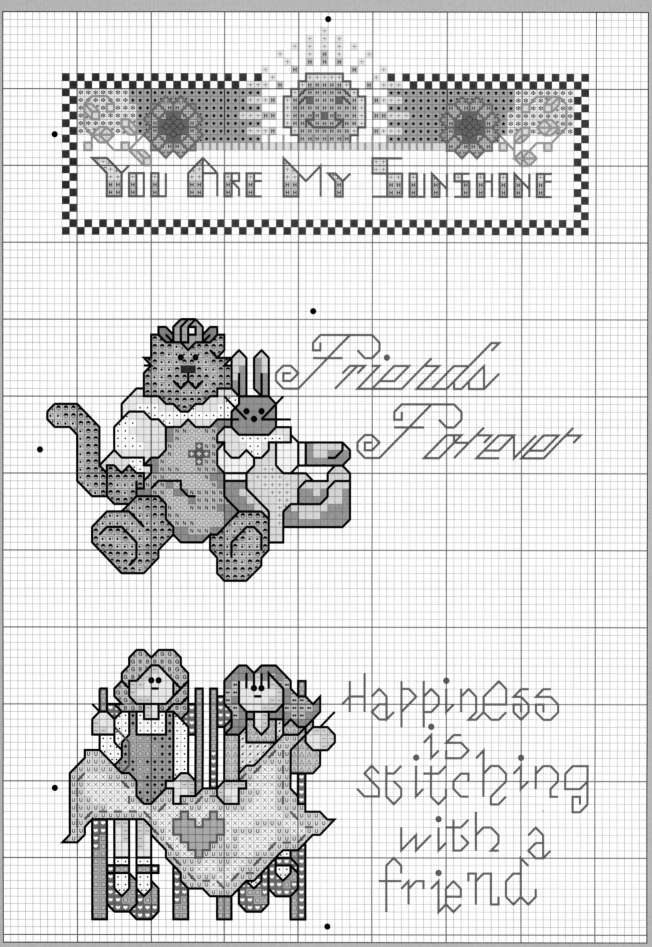

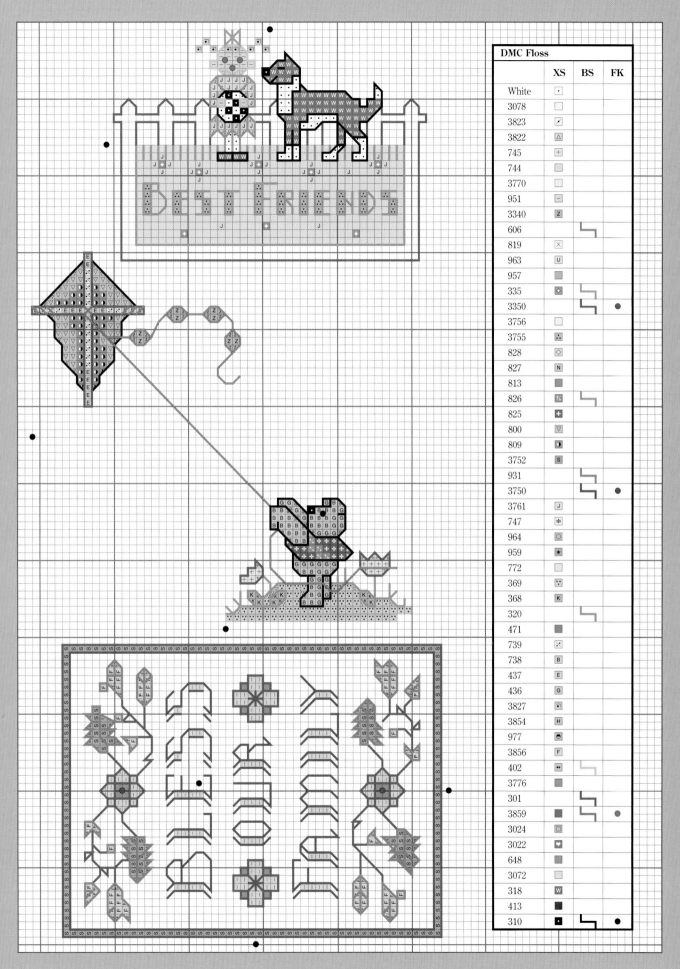

DMC Floss			
	XS	BS	FK
White	·		
3078	☐		
3823	◿		
3822	△		
745	+		
744	☐		
3770	☐		
951	⊟		
3340	Z		
606		⌐	
819	✕		
963	U		
957	▦		
335	◈	⌐	
3350		⌐	●
3756	☐		
3755	∷		
828	◇		
827	N		
813	▦		
826	▩	⌐	
825	✚		
800	▽		
809	◑		
3752	S		
931		⌐	
3750		⌐	●
3761	J		
747	✳		
964	○		
959	★		
772	☐		
369	∷		
368	K		
320		⌐	
471	▦		
739	✕		
738	B		
437	E		
436	G		
3827	◨		
3854	H		
977	◕		
3856	F		
402	◖	⌐	
3776	▦		
301		⌐	
3859	■	⌐	●
3024	▥		
3022	♥		
648	▦		
3072	☐		
318	W		
413	▦		
310	■	⌐	●

YESTERDAY IS HISTORY
TOMORROW IS A MYSTERY
TODAY IS A GIFT
THAT'S WHY WE CALL IT
THE PRESENT

A Friend
is a
Present
you give
yourself

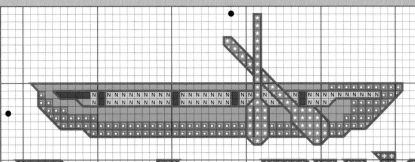

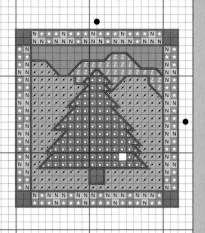

Dads Rule

Sisters

MOM:

A cherished friend
and personal cheerleader
who will always see you
through
rose-colored glasses.

DMC Floss			
	XS	BS	FK
White	·		
3823	☐		
677	+		
676	K		
744	☐		
743	⊡		
741	☐		
783	Z		
3354	⊟		
893	✳		
957	☐		
225	☐		
223	▣		
3721		⌐	
211	☐		
210	◪		
554	◖		
553		⌐	●
340	✚		
3756	☐		
775	⠶		
827	☐		
3755	◈		
809	▦		
825		⌐	
798	E		
797	▪		
704	△		
702	▣		
700		⌐	
563	▣		
562	⊙		
561	▪		
3855	U		
738	N		
3827	○	⌐	
976		⌐	
3776	✦		
3772	▣		
400		⌐	
317		⌐	

When a child is born
so is
a grandparent

MY GRANDCHILDREN
ARE
ANGELS

Baby's first
Haircut

World's Greatest
MOM
GRANDMA

A B C D E F G H I J K
L M N O P Q R S T U
V W X Y Z abcdefghij
klmnopqrstuvwxyz

Outstanding
Aunt
Award

To: Aunt Marcie

DMC Floss			
	XS	BS	FK
White	·		
746	□		
745	◿		
744	□		
743	U		
742	⊡		
3078	✕		
3823	−		
3822	⦂		
3820		⌐	
948	□		
963	+	⌐	○
3708	□		
957	E		
351	■		
3609	□		
3608	▧		
3608 } 3607	■		
718		⌐	
554	▦		
552		⌐	●
333		⌐	
340	■		
747	□		
3761	△		
3766	■		
826		⌐	
813	Z		
799	✳		
772	□		
955	H		
954	▣		
913	✷		
562	▨		
561		⌐	
3855	◎		
976		⌐	
3776	■		
301		⌐	
762	□		
415	✳		
318	■		
317		⌐	●
310			●

FAMILY VACATION

FAMILY RETREAT

My Dad's the BEST!

Swings are Double Fun!

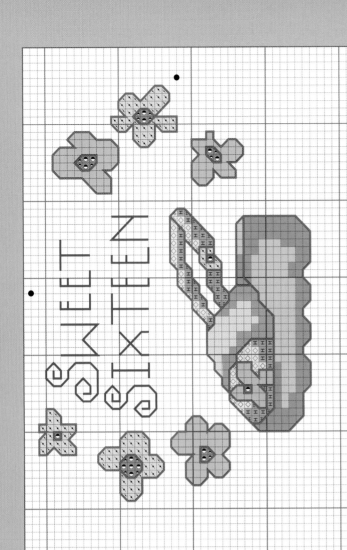

DMC Floss	XS	BS	DMC Floss	XS	BS	FK
White	·		798		⌐	●
744	↗		747	◇		
677	▫		959	H		
676	▪		3813	U		
948	▫		503		⌐	
3341	▪		3816	✚		
351	✳		772	▫		
350	E		955	∴		
349	■		954	▪		
818	−		913	▣		
3716	◎		562	✱		
961	✚		561		⌐	
3350		⌐	950	▪		
211	▫		3064	▨		
554	▪		3855	⊡		
3761	+		3827	N		
828	▫		402	↗		
3755	Z	⌐	976		⌐	
3325	⊡		3776	▽		
813	◑		975		⌐	
334	■		318	▪		
322		⌐	317	♥	⌐	●
799	★					

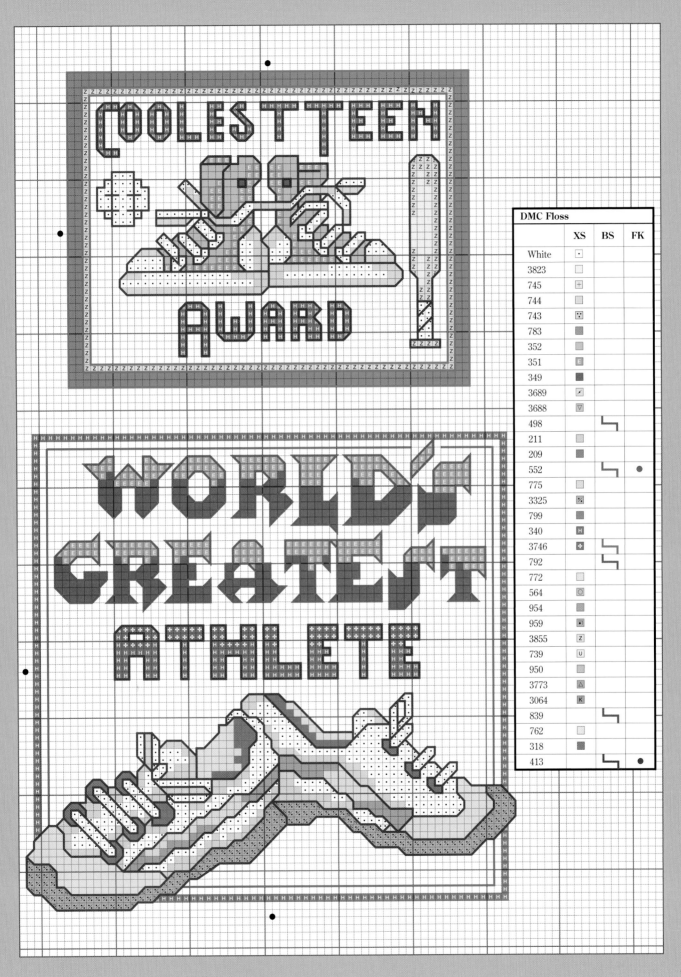

DMC Floss			
	XS	BS	FK
White	⋅		
3823	☐		
745	+		
744	☐		
743	⊡		
783	☐		
352	☐		
351	E		
349	☐		
3689	◿		
3688	▽		
498		⌐	
211	☐		
209	☐		
552		⌐	●
775	☐		
3325	▨		
799	☐		
340	H		
3746	✚	⌐	
792		⌐	
772	☐		
564	◎		
954	☐		
959	▪		
3855	Z		
739	U		
950	☐		
3773	△		
3064	K		
839		⌐	
762	☐		
318	☐		
413		⌐	●

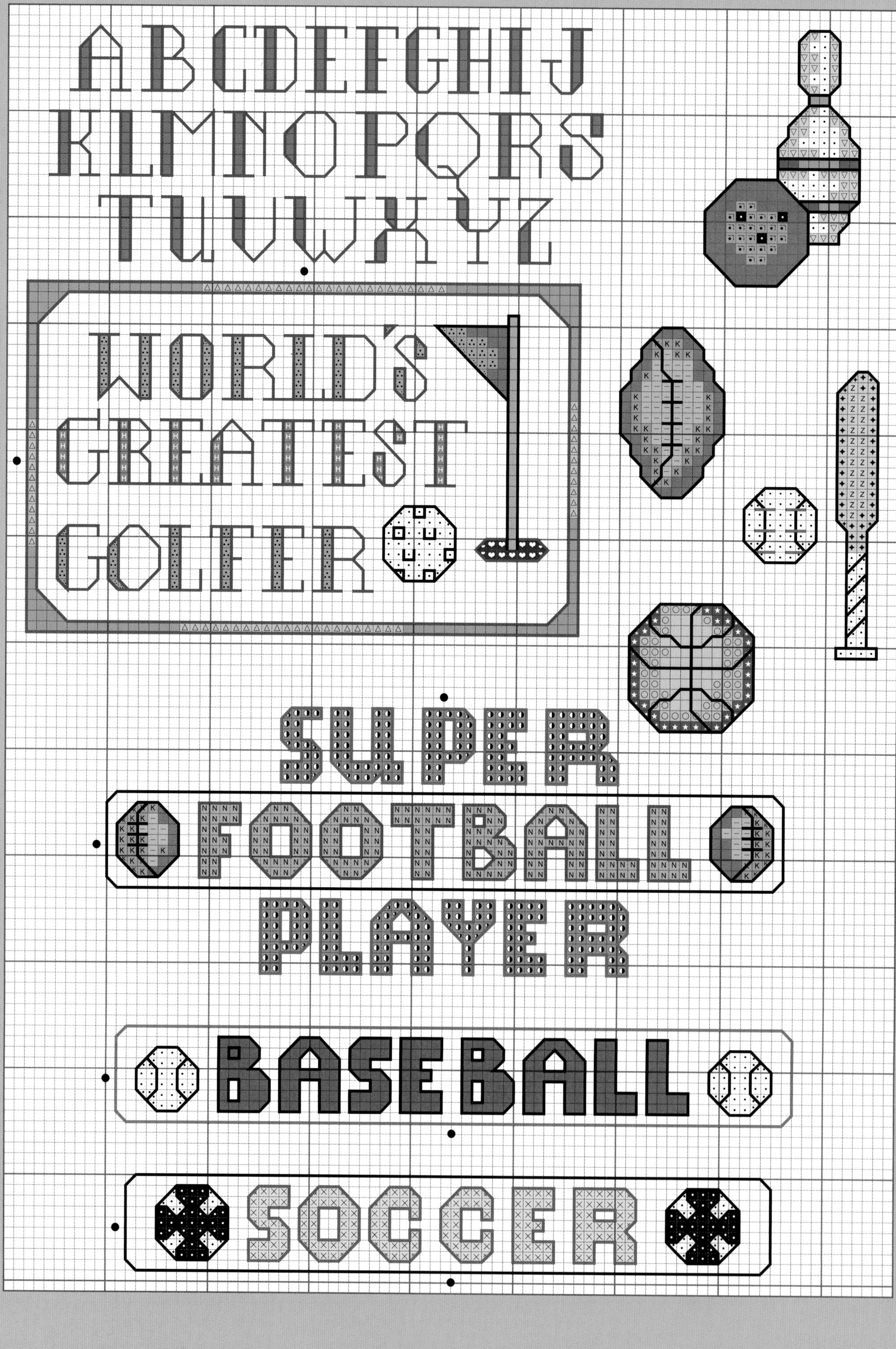

ABCDEFGHIJ
KLMNOPQRS
TUVWXYZ

WORLD'S
GREATEST
GOLFER

SUPER
FOOTBALL
PLAYER

BASEBALL

SOCCER

40

DMC Floss			DMC Floss			
	XS	BS		XS	BS	FK
White	·		562	■		
727	☐		561		⌐	
744	✕		3816	H		
676	△		989	✦		
729	■		739	◇		
945	☐		738	Z		
352	◢		437	✴		
351	■		436	✚		
350	▨		950	−		
349	■	⌐	3773	■		
605	☐		3064	K		
3609	✛		3772	■		
3608	▨		3863	N		
3607	■		839		⌐	
554	E		402	◯		
828	☐		301	★	⌐	
775	▽		3072	J		
800	U		762	☐		
813	◑		415	▨		
826	■		318	▨		
825		⌐	317	G	⌐	
772	☐		413	♥		
954	▨		310	■	⌐	●
563	■					

Bless
Our
Home

Bless Our Home Sampler

DMC Floss				
	XS	BS	FK	LS
White	·	⌐		
3823	▫			
3855	◪			
726	▫			
783	◼			
741	◉			
353	▫			
352	▨			
351	◼			
603	⁙			
718	◼			
915	✛	⌐		
210	◼			
208	△			
550	E	⌐		
3753	▭			
800	▫			
809	▣			
798	◼			
3766	H			
806	⁙	⌐		
3348	▫			
988	✚			
986	◼	⌐		
3813	Z			
3816	◼			
3847	◙	⌐		
3826	N	⌐		╲
435	▽			
434	◐			
919	★	⌐		
842	▦			
841	✦			
839	◼	⌐		
762	▫			
318	U			
317	◼	⌐		
310	▪	⌐	●	╲

44

HOME
SWEET
HOME

Home, that spot of earth supremely

Home Sweet Home

blessed; a dearer, sweeter spot than

all the rest.

DMC Floss				
	XS	BS	FK	LS
White	·	⌐		
3823	☐			
3855	◪			
726	☐			
783	■			
741	◎			
353	☐			
352	▨			
351	☐			
603	⊡			
718	■			
915	✚	⌐		
210	☐			
208	△			
550	E	⌐		
3753	⊟			
800	☐			
809	▣			
798	■			
3766	H			
806	⊡	⌐		
3348	☐			
988	✚			
986	■	⌐		
3813	Z			
3816	■			
3847	◙	⌐		
3826	N	⌐		╲
435	▽			
434	◖			
919	★	⌐		
842	■			
841	✦			
839	■	⌐		
762	☐			
318	U			
317	■	⌐		
310	▪	⌐	●	╲

Mi Casa

No matter what, no matter w

Wherever you wander, wherever you

My Huis

is there.

place like home.

DMC Floss				
	XS	**BS**	**FK**	**LS**
White	·	⌐		
3823	☐			
3855	✗			
726	☐			
783	■			
741	◎			
353	☐			
352	⚿			
351	☐			
603	▦			
718	■			
915	✚	⌐		
210	☐			
208	△			
550	E	⌐		
3753	⊟			
800	☐			
809	▣			
798	■			
3766	H			
806	▦	⌐		
3348	☐			
988	✚			
986	■	⌐		
3813	Z			
3816	▨			
3847	▣	⌐		
3826	N	⌐		╱
435	▽			
434	◖			
919	★	⌐		
842	▦			
841	✚			
839	■	⌐		
762	☐			
318	U			
317	■	⌐		
310	▪	⌐	●	╲

Bottom Left

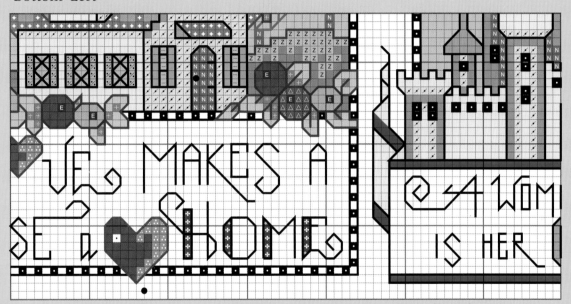

Bottom Center

Bottom Right

51

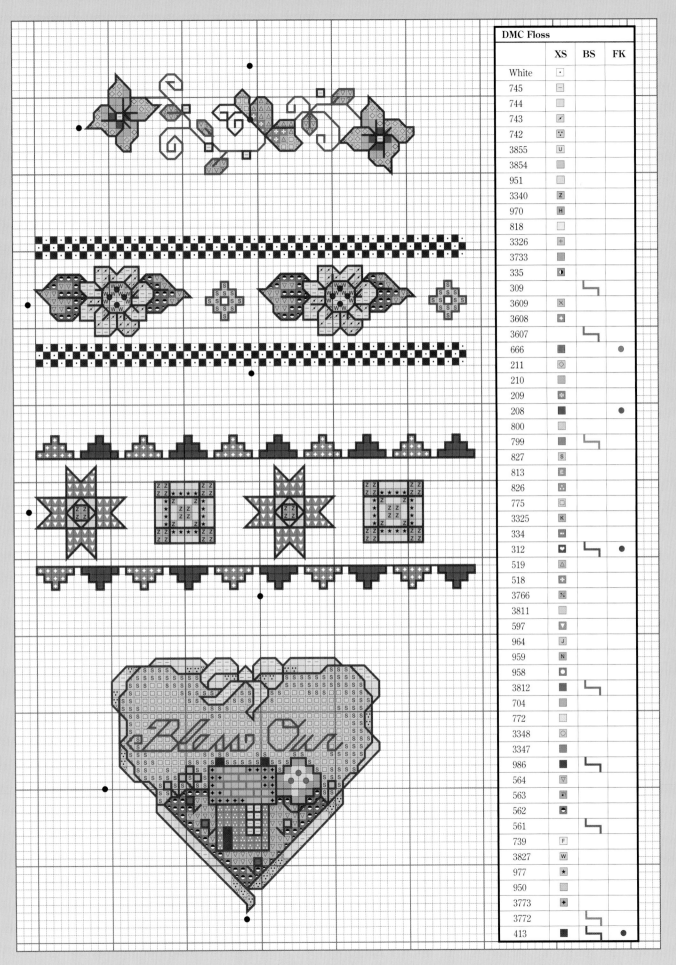

DMC Floss			
	XS	BS	FK
White	·		
745	⊟		
744	▨		
743	◪		
742	⦂		
3855	U		
3854	▢		
951	▢		
3340	Z		
970	H		
818	▢		
3326	+		
3733	▨		
335	◐		
309		⌐	
3609	×		
3608	⊞		
3607		⌐	
666	▦		●
211	◇		
210	▨		
209	✿		
208	▦		●
800	▨		
799	▨	⌐	
827	S		
813	E		
826	▦		
775	▢		
3325	K		
334	⊡		
312	♥	⌐	●
519	△		
518	⊞		
3766	▨		
3811	▢		
597	▽		
964	J		
959	N		
958	▣		
3812	▦	⌐	
704	▨		
772	▢		
3348	○		
3347	▨		
986	▦	⌐	
564	▽		
563	▪		
562	▣		
561		⌐	
739	F		
3827	W		
977	★		
950	▨		
3773	✦		
3772		⌐	
413	▦	⌐	●

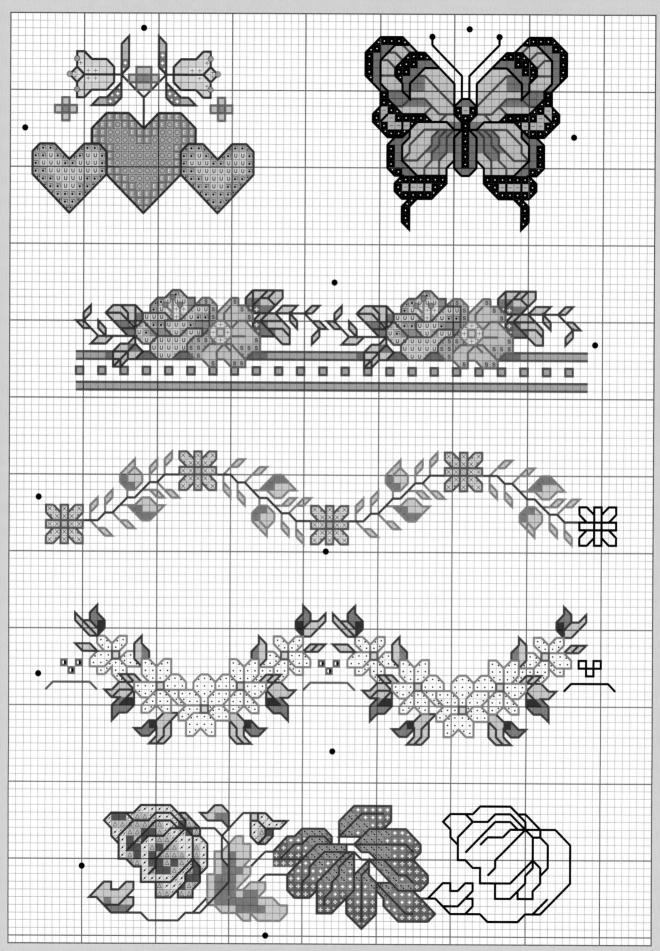

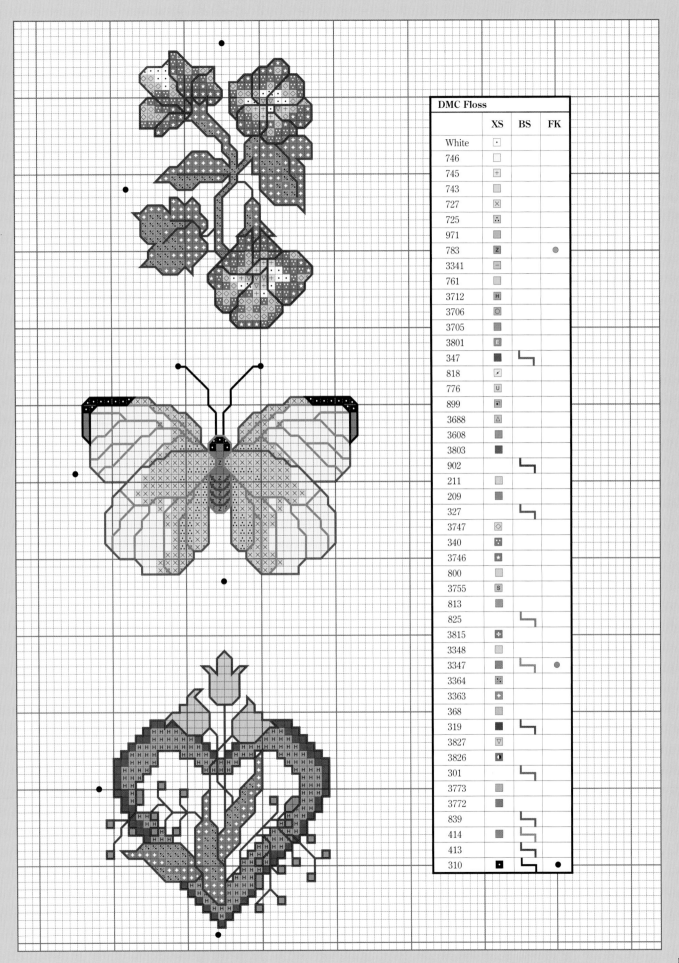

DMC Floss			
	XS	BS	FK
White	·		
746	▫		
745	+		
743	▫		
727	⊠		
725	⠶		
971	▪		
783	Z		●
3341	−		
761	▫		
3712	H		
3706	◎		
3705	▪		
3801	E		
347	■	⌐	
818	✓		
776	U		
899	◙		
3688	△		
3608	▪		
3803	▪		
902		⌐	
211	▫		
209	▪		
327		⌐	
3747	◈		
340	∷		
3746	★		
800	▫		
3755	S		
813	▪		
825		⌐	
3815	✚		
3348	▫		
3347	▪	⌐	●
3364	⅗		
3363	✚		
368	▫		
319	■	⌐	
3827	▽		
3826	◑		
301		⌐	
3773	▪		
3772	▪		
839		⌐	
414	▪	⌐	
413		⌐	
310	■	⌐	●

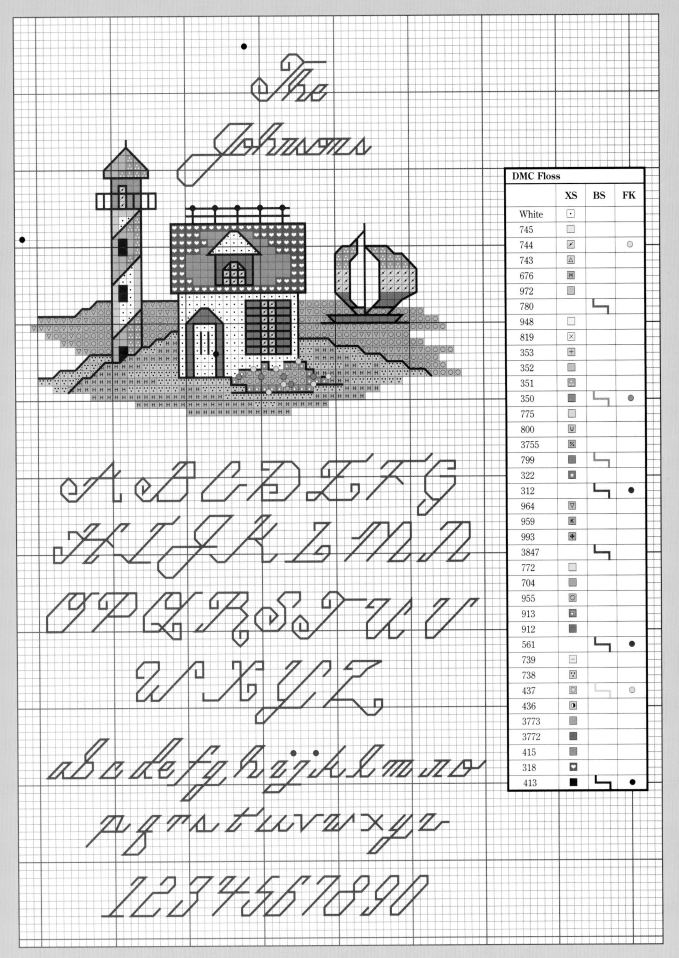

DMC Floss			
	XS	BS	FK
White	·		
745			
744			○
743	△		
676	H		
972			
780		⌐	
948			
819	×		
353	+		
352			
351			
350		⌐	●
775			
800	U		
3755			
799		⌐	
322			
312		⌐	●
964	▽		
959	K		
993			
3847		⌐	
772			
704			
955	○		
913			
912			
561		⌐	●
739	−		
738			
437	□	⌐	○
436			
3773			
3772			
415			
318			
413	■	⌐	●

QUEEN ANNE

DMC Floss			
	XS	BS	FK
White	·		
746			
745	−		
744			
3823	⊠		
676	Z		
729		⌐	
783	⠨		
3047	⠳		
760	✳		
3328	◖		
335		⌐	
326	■	⌐	●
818			
3727	⊙		
224			
223	✚		
3721	▲		
3803	■		
3687	⊠		
902	★	⌐	
775			
3325	H		
334	✚		
322	⠶		
312	■	⌐	
964	◇		
372	■		
3012	K		
369			
368	E		
367	■	⌐	
3348	J		
3347	⠶		
986	✦	⌐	
3855	U		
3854			
3827	△	⌐	
976	■		
975	⠳		
738	S		
437	N		
435	G	⌐	●
433	■		
3772	⠪		
842			
840	⠶		
839	◘	⌐	
647	F̄		
844	■	⌐	●
762			
415	■	⌐	

DMC Floss			
	XS	BS	FK
White	·		
3823	▫		
744	▬		
727	▫		
725	△		
3855	+		
783	▨		
781		⌐	
970	N		
818	▫		
3326	▨		
963	◪		
961	▨		
957	H		
3354	U		
3688	◫		
335		⌐	●
606	◎		
666	✚		
498	▨	⌐	
211	▫		
210	◫		
209	▨		
3837		⌐	●
3743	▣		
3042	△		
800	E		
3755	▨		
322	◫		
312		⌐	
794	✺		
797	■		
747	▫		
964	▨		
958		⌐	
504	J		
503	◐		
955	▨		
913	◪		
562	▨		
561		⌐	
3348	▫		
3347	▨	⌐	●
986	■	⌐	●
762	▫		
415	▨		
414	✺	⌐	
535	■	⌐	

DMC Floss			
	XS	BS	FK
White	·		
712			
3823	⊠		
3078			
745	−		
744			
743	⊘		◯
742	⦂		
676	H		
3855	⟋		
741			
950			
3779	+		
3778	K		
776			
899	E		
3712			
351	Z		
349	✳		●
347	■	⌐	
210			
208	■		●
800			
3755	⊙		
598	S		
597	◑		
3810	■		
504			
3816		⌐	
564	▢		
563			
562	⊞		
561		⌐	●
523	▧		
3348			
3347	▨		
3346		⌐	
738	U		
437	⠇		
3827	N		
976	◖	⌐	
3773	△		
3772	■		
842	J		
841	▼		
3863	⊡		
3862	⬧		
839		⌐	
632	■	⌐	
647	◖		
762			
415	▽		
414	■	⌐	
318	✦		
3799		⌐	●

DMC Floss			
	XS	BS	FK
White	·		
746	☐		
745	−	⌐	
744	▨		
743	◇		
3823	☒		
677	U		
950	▨		
3778	◪		
758	+		
3341	▨		
722	▨		
3708	☐		
352	▽		
350	▦		
347	✚		
817		⌐	
3326	○		
309	▦		
815	■	⌐	
3609	Z		
3607	▦		
3747	☐		
340	▦		
3746	▦		
800	▢		
813	▦		
826	✚		
825		⌐	●
368	▨		
367	E		
3348	△		
3347	▦		
986	■	⌐	●
738	J		
437	✳		
436	☐		
435	▣		
433	■	⌐	
422	S		
3828	H		
420		⌐	
3856	✚		
402	K		
3776	▨		
3826	★		
355		⌐	●
3072	⁒		
762	☐		
415	M	⌐	
414	▦		
318	▲		
413	■	⌐	●

WINDMILL

LIGHTHOUSE

DMC Floss			
	XS	BS	FK
White	·		
3823			
744	+		
742			○
725			
783	◎		
947			
3326			
3712	E		
347	■	⌐	●
224			
223	U		
3722	✦		
605	◢		
3608			
211			
209			
828	J		
827	Z		
826		⌐	
775	–		
3325			
3755	△		
799	◫		
798	◪		
312	■	⌐	●
3752	⁒		
931	◑		
3766	H		
964	S		
959	✦	⌐	
563	◫		
955	◇		
913	★		
912		⌐	
992	◕		
504			
503	N		
3812	■	⌐	
3809	♥		
543	✕		
3864			
738	◻		
437	K		
3772	✸		
3826		⌐	
318	▽		
414	◫	⌐	
317	◕		
3799	■	⌐	●

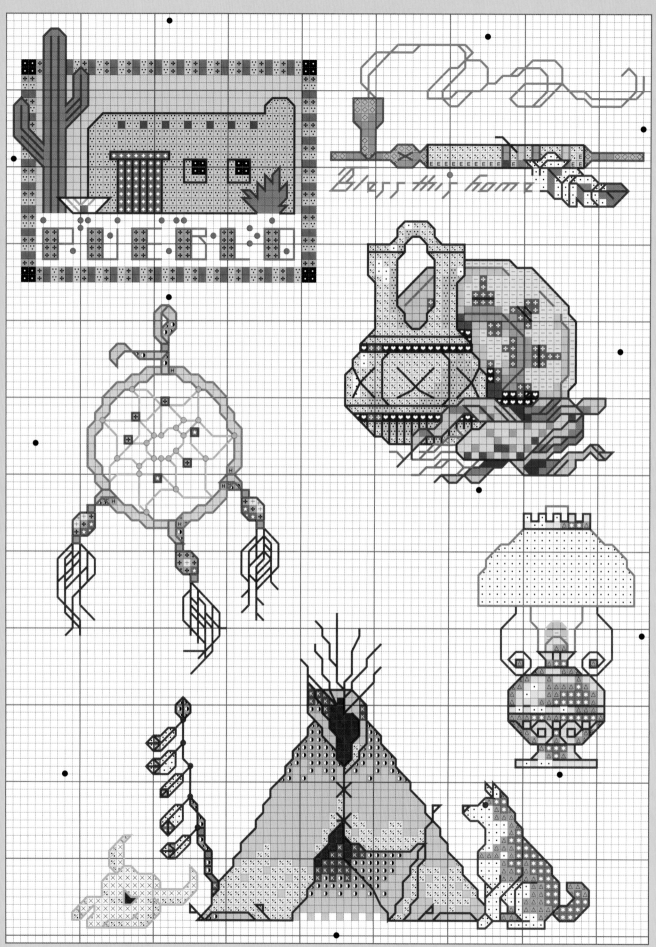

Bless this home

DMC Floss			
	XS	**BS**	**FK**
White	·		
Ecru	×		
727			
725			
780	Z		
3855			
3854		⌐	
758	◇		
3778			
351			
817		⌐	●
3608			
3607		⌐	
211			
828			
334	◎		
798			
312		⌐	
747	+		
964	▽		
3766	✚		
3760	★		
3812		⌐	
913			
910	◧		
3348			
3347		⌐	
986		⌐	
739	⊠		
738	⊡		
437	E		
433			
3826		⌐	●
3774			
3773	H		
3772	✚	⌐	
3830		⌐	
632	▼		
3864			
3863	◑	⌐	●
841			
840	✚	⌐	
839	K		
838	♥	⌐	
762			
415	△	⌐	
318			
414	✳	⌐	●
413		⌐	●
310	◼		

Bless This House

DMC Floss			
	XS	BS	FK
White	·		
3823			
744			
3855			
3854	△		
945			
3341	+		
722	K		
3328	H		
351			
606			
818			
3326	U		
335	+		
498		⌐	
3722			
221		⌐	
775			
800			
813			
799			
955	○		
913			
772			
989			
988			
987			
986		⌐	
3348	−		
3347	E		
3813	▽		
3816			
959 958 }	○		
958		⌐	
3847		⌐	●
436	J		
3776	△		
3827	Z		
977			
976			
3826			
975		⌐	
841			
839		⌐	
318	N	⌐	
414			
413		⌐	●
310	■	⌐	●

71

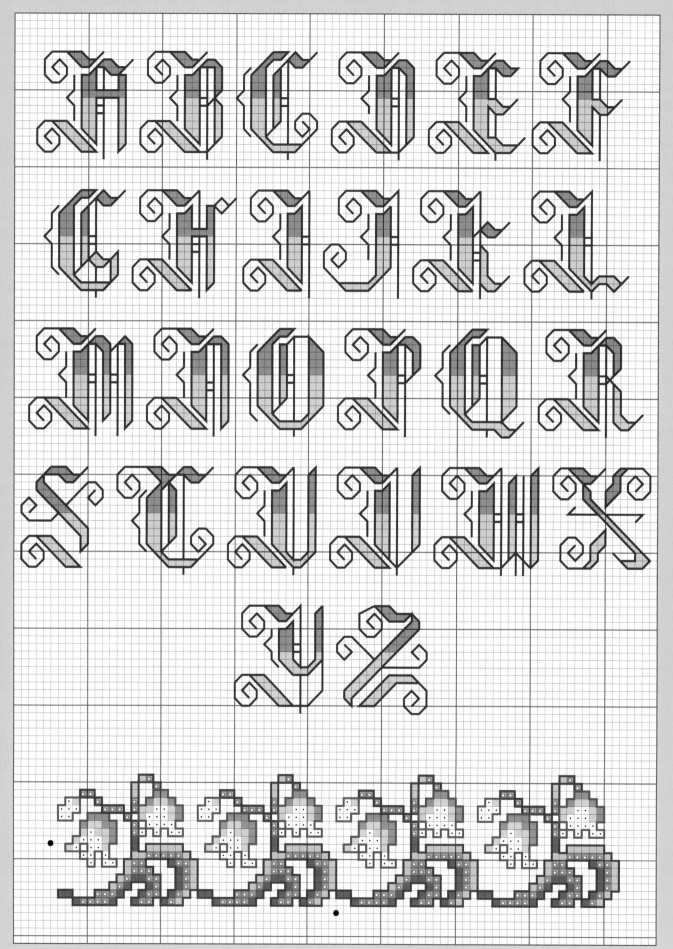

72

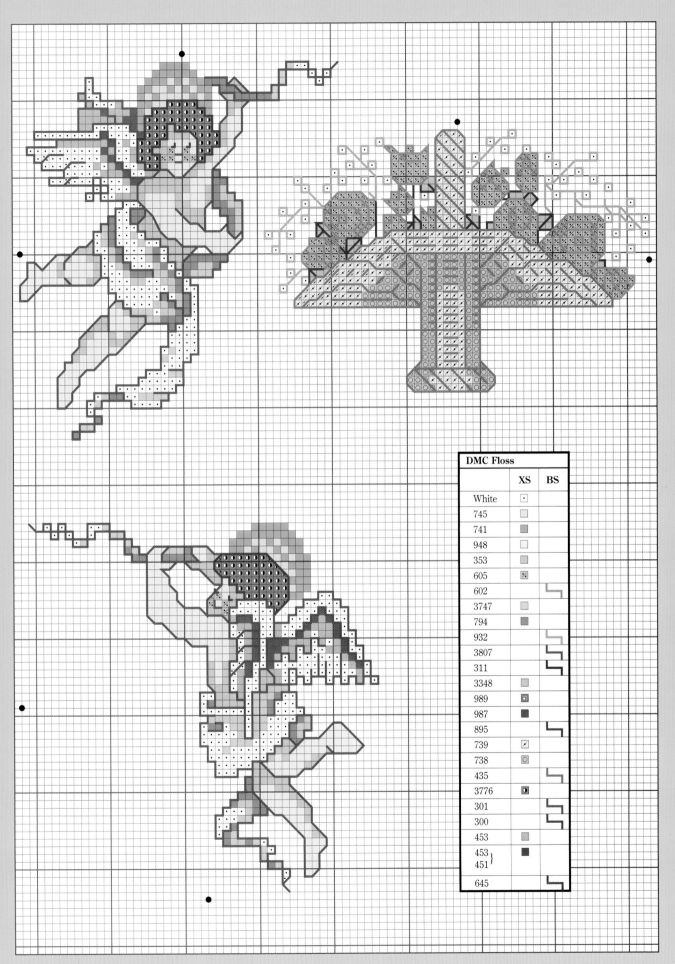

DMC Floss		
	XS	BS
White	·	
745		
741		
948		
353		
605		
602		
3747		
794		
932		
3807		
311		
3348		
989		
987		
895		
739		
738		
435		
3776		
301		
300		
453		
453 } 451		
645		

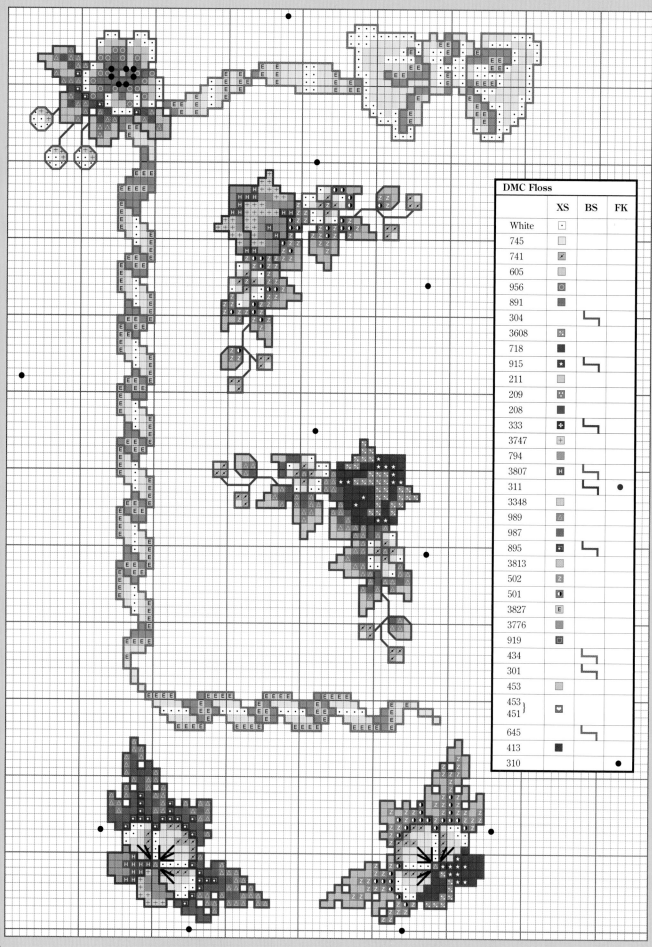

DMC Floss			
	XS	BS	FK
White	⊡		
745	▧		
741	▨		
605	▦		
956	◎		
891	▰		
304		⌐	
3608	▨		
718	▰		
915	★	⌐	
211	▢		
209	▨		
208	▰		
333	✠	⌐	
3747	＋		
794	▰		
3807	H	⌐	
311		⌐	●
3348	▨		
989	◿		
987	▰		
895	▣	⌐	
3813	▦		
502	Z		
501	◑		
3827	E		
3776	▰		
919	▣		
434		⌐	
301		⌐	
453	▦		
453 } 451	♥		
645		⌐	
413	▰		
310			●

Alphabet and numbers can be found on page 57.

Alphabet and numbers
can be found on page 57.

DMC Floss			
	XS	**BS**	**FK**
White	·		
712			
745	−		
742	U		
727	◿		
676	△		
780		⌐	
754	+		
758			
950	∴		
3778			
352	Z		
351	⊘		
350	✚		
817			
606	✕		
963			
957			
321	E	⌐	
3755			
3325	▣	⌐	
809	N		
334	▦		
825		⌐	
989			
3363	▽		
3053	K		
772			
954	◖		
913			
3813			
503	H		
3816	▣		
562	◆		
561		⌐	●
928	J		
739	◇		
738	S		
437	↔		
3827	✕		
3825	F		
402	▣		
922	✦		
3776	⊘		
407	●	⌐	
3772	✶		
632	▪		
841	▼		
839		⌐	●
415	▨		
318	▣		
414	◨		
310	◼	⌐	●

Bless
Our
Children

Bless Our Children Sampler

<table>

DMC Floss	XS	BS	FK
White	·		
712	−		
3823	□		
745	△		
744	□		
743	✚		
948 353 }	↗		
3824	□		
3341	E		
351	■	⌐	●
818	□		
776	○		
899	▪		
335		⌐	●
211	+		
210	■		
553		⌐	●
3841	▨		
3755	■		
322		⌐	
964	∴		
959	✦	⌐	
955	■		
954	H		
913	◐		
3815		⌐	●
945	□		
402	★		
739	∵		
436	N		
975		⌐	
415	■		
414	◙		
317		⌐	
310	▪	⌐	●

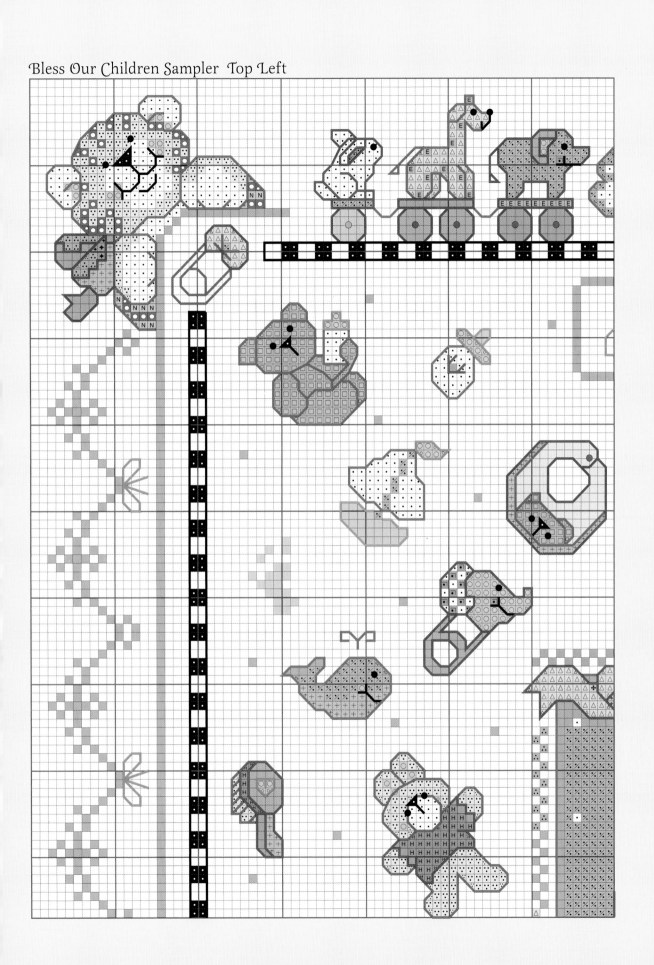

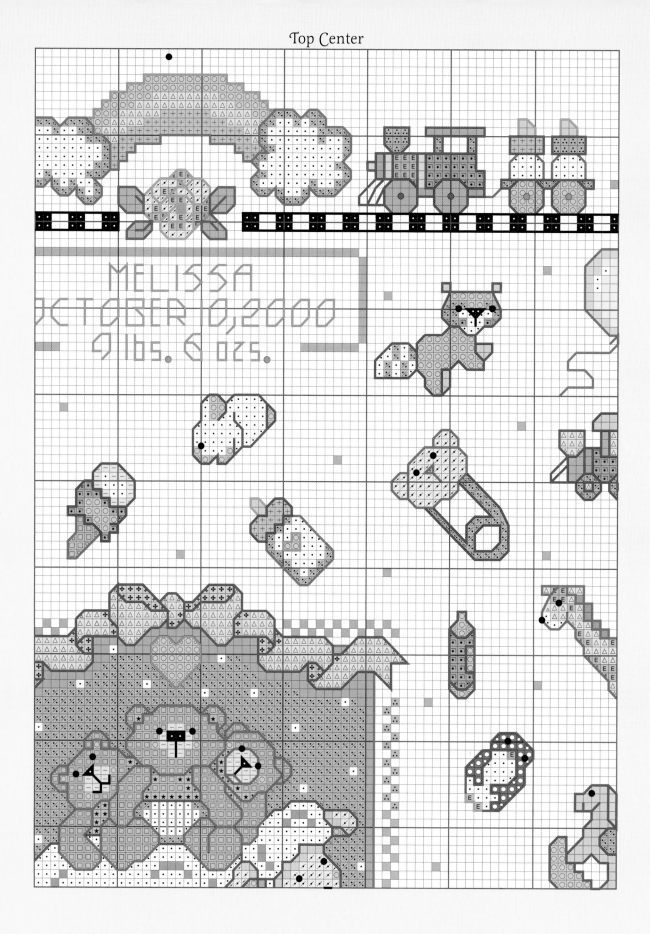

MELISSA
OCTOBER 10, 2000
9 lbs. 6 ozs.

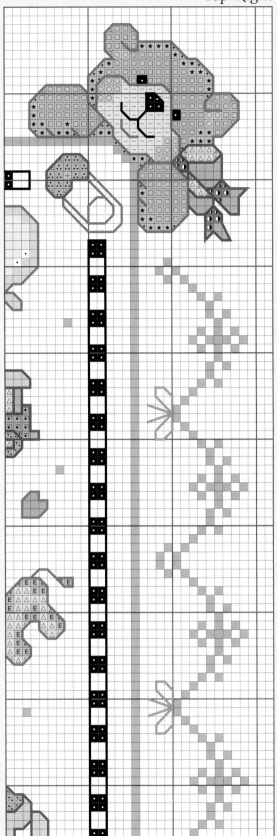

DMC Floss			
	XS	**BS**	**FK**
White	·		
712	−		
3823	▢		
745	△		
744	▣		
743	✦		
948 } 353	✎		
3824	▢		
3341	E		
351	▣	⌐	●
818	▢		
776	○		
899	▣		
335		⌐	●
211	+		
210	▣		
553		⌐	●
3841	⊠		
3755	▣		
322		⌐	
964	⋰		
959	✦	⌐	
955	▣		
954	H		
913	◑		
3815		⌐	●
945	▢		
402	★		
739	⋰		
436	N		
975		⌐	
415	▣		
414	◙		
317		⌐	
310	▪	⌐	●

Middle Right

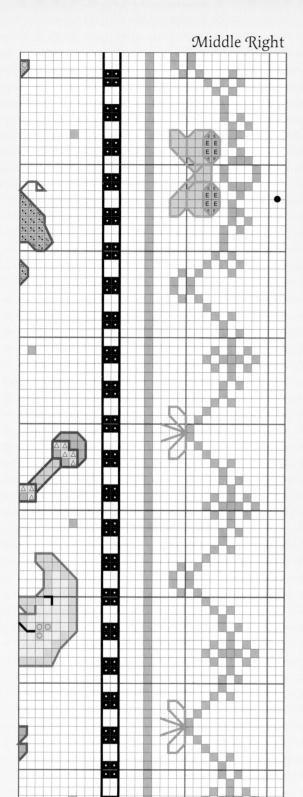

DMC Floss			
	XS	BS	FK
White	·		
712	▬		
3823	▢		
745	△		
744	▦		
743	✦		
948 } 353	✎		
3824	▦		
3341	E		
351	▦	⌐	●
818	▢		
776	○		
899	▣		
335		⌐	●
211	✚		
210	▦		
553		⌐	●
3841	▦		
3755	▦		
322		⌐	
964	▦		
959	✦	⌐	
955	▦		
954	H		
913	◑		
3815		⌐	●
945	▢		
402	★		
739	⁞		
436	N		
975		⌐	
415	▦		
414	◘		
317		⌐	
310	▣	⌐	●

86

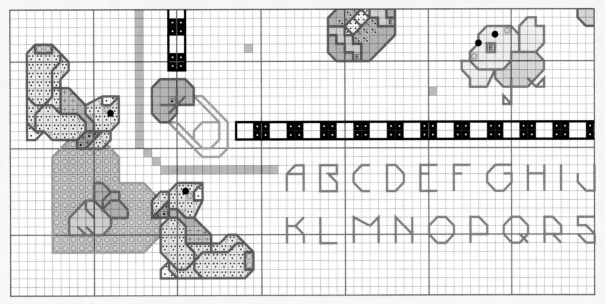

Bottom Left

A B C D E F G H I J
K L M N O P Q R S

T U V W X Y Z
1 2 3 4 5 6 7 8 9 0

Bottom Center

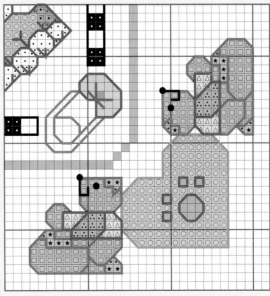

Bottom Right

Bless our Godchild

Bless Our Littlest Angel

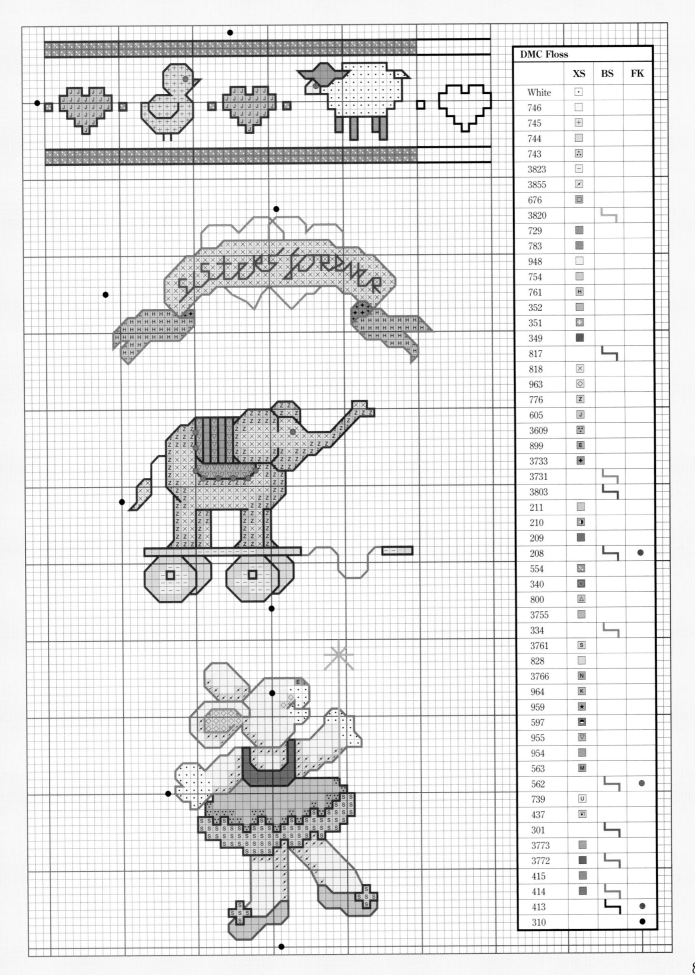

DMC Floss			
	XS	**BS**	**FK**
White	·		
746			
745	+		
744			
743	::		
3823	−		
3855	∕		
676	▣		
3820		⌐	
729	▦		
783	▦		
948			
754			
761	H		
352	▦		
351	+		
349	▦		
817		⌐	
818	⊠		
963	◇		
776	Z		
605	J		
3609	::		
899	E		
3733	✦		
3731		⌐	
3803		⌐	
211	▦		
210	◑		
209	▦		
208		⌐	●
554	▨		
340	◉		
800	△		
3755	▦		
334		⌐	
3761	S		
828			
3766	N		
964	K		
959	★		
597	◐		
955	▽		
954	▦		
563	M		
562		⌐	●
739	U		
437	▣		
301		⌐	
3773	▦		
3772	▦	⌐	
415	▦		
414	▦	⌐	
413		⌐	●
310			●

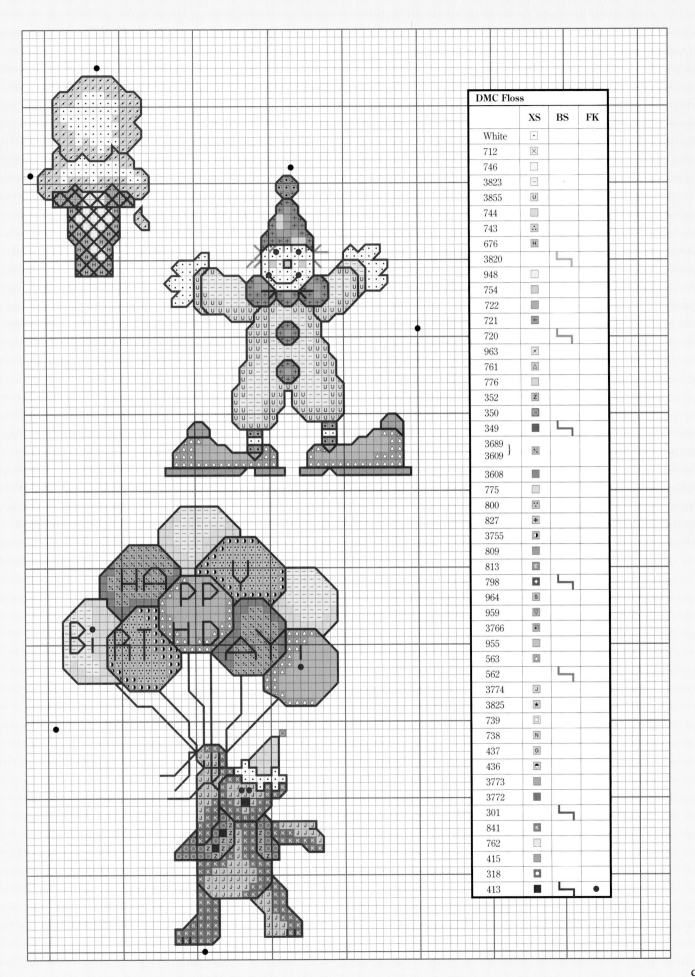

DMC Floss			
	XS	BS	FK
White	·		
712	⊠		
746	☐		
3823	⊟		
3855	U		
744	▦		
743	⠇		
676	H		
3820		⌐	
948	☐		
754	▦		
722	▦		
721	✚		
720		⌐	
963	⟋		
761	△		
776	▦		
352	Z		
350	◉		
349	■	⌐	
3689 } 3609	⠢		
3608	▦		
775	☐		
800	⠢		
827	✚		
3755	◑		
809	▦		
813	E		
798	✦	⌐	
964	S		
959	▽		
3766	▪		
955	▦		
563	△		
562		⌐	
3774	J		
3825	★		
739	☐		
738	N		
437	G		
436	◣		
3773	▦		
3772	▦		
301		⌐	
841	K		
762	☐		
415	▦		
318	◙		
413	■	⌐	●

91

DMC Floss			
	XS	BS	FK
White	·		
712	◢		
3823	☐		
745	⊟		
743	▧		
3855	△		
3854	▨		
948	☐		
945	▨		
754	⊞		
352	▨		
351	⊠		
350	▦		
349	▨		
666	E	⌐	
963	☒		
3326	◎		
335	⊕		
309		⌐	
3609	Z		
341	▨		
340	▣		
775	▨		
800	∴		
3755	▣		
813	▣		
799	H		
798	▲	⌐	
3761	◇		
772	☐		
704	▨		
955	S		
739	U		
437	✳		
3824	J		
3825	▽		
3827	N		
402	◗		
3776	▨		
400		⌐	
3773	▨		
3772	◘	⌐	
841	K		
839	▨		
838	★	⌐	
415	▨		
414	⊞		
413	▦	⌐	●
310	▣	⌐	●

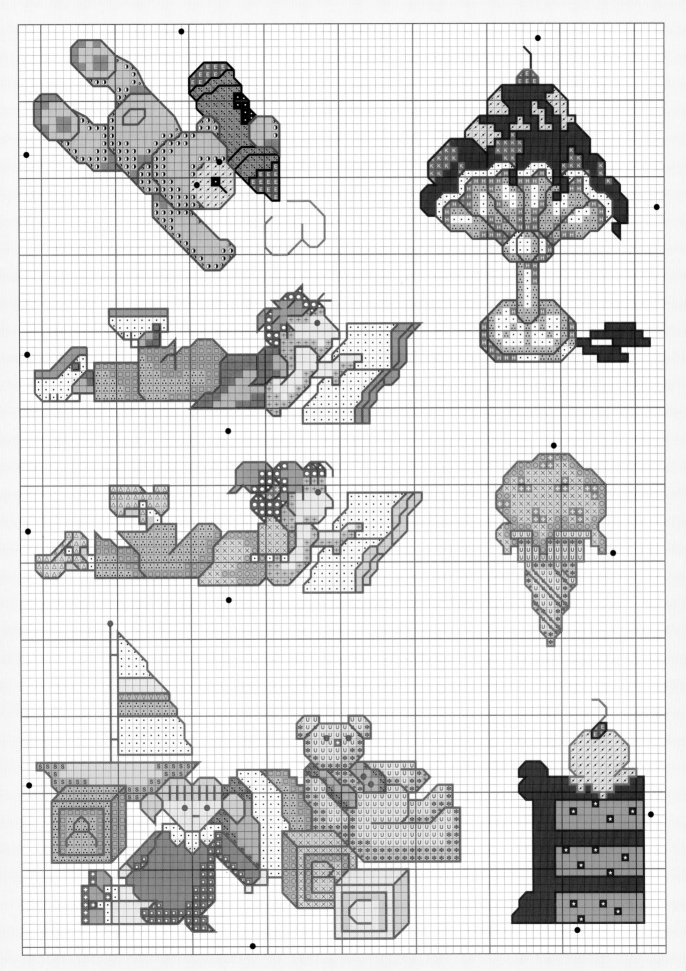

ABCDEFGHIJ
KLMNOPQR
STUVWXYZ

MICHAEL'S
ROOM

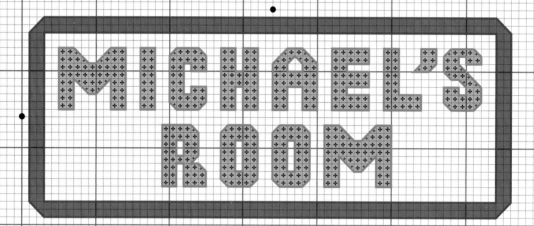

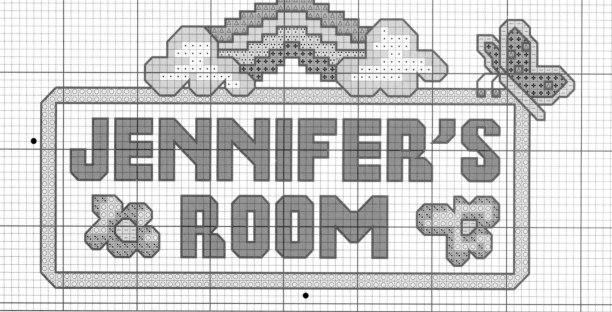

JENNIFER'S
ROOM

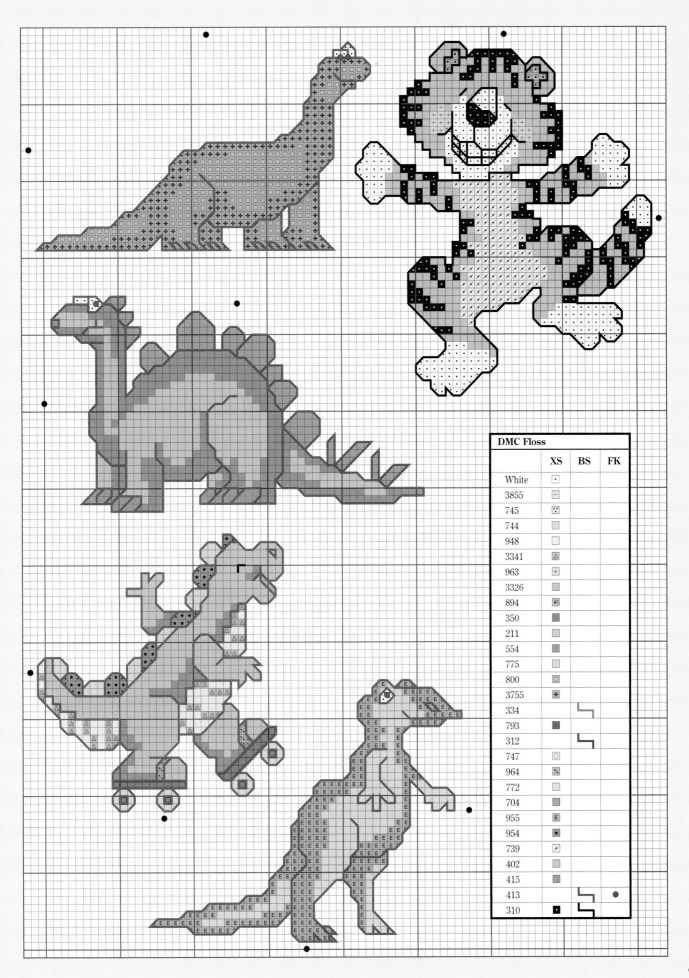

DMC Floss			
	XS	BS	FK
White	·		
3855	−		
745	∷		
744	▫		
948	□		
3341	△		
963	+		
3326	▨		
894	⊡		
350	■		
211	▢		
554	▥		
775	▫		
800	▢		
3755	✚		
334		⌐	
793	■		
312		⌐	
747	○		
964	∷		
772	□		
704	▨		
955	E		
954	★		
739	◿		
402	▨		
415	▨		
413		⌐	●
310	▪	⌐	

Our Bundle of Love

It's a Girl!

It's a Boy!

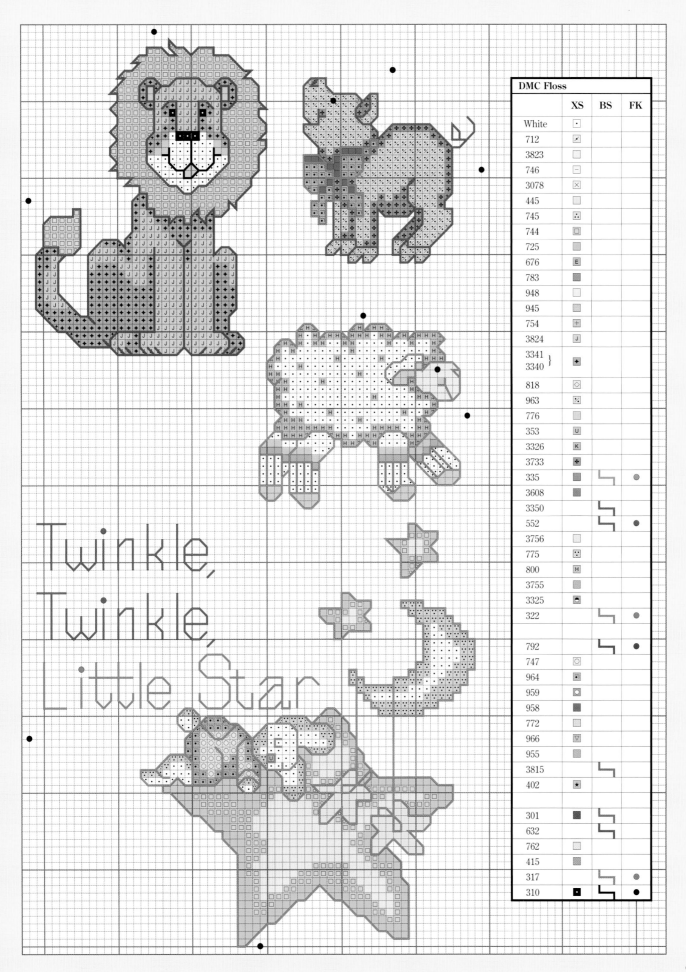

DMC Floss			
	XS	BS	FK
White	·		
712	⊿		
3823	☐		
746	−		
3078	⊠		
445	☐		
745	⦂		
744	▢		
725	▥		
676	E		
783	▦		
948	☐		
945	▨		
754	+		
3824	J		
3341 ⎫ 3340 ⎭	✦		
818	◇		
963	⦂		
776	▦		
353	U		
3326	K		
3733	✚		
335	▥	⌐	●
3608	▥		
3350		⌐	
552		⌐	●
3756	☐		
775	⦂		
800	H		
3755	▦		
3325	◖		
322		⌐	●
792		⌐	●
747	⊘		
964	⊡		
959	◉		
958	■		
772	☐		
966	▽		
955	▨		
3815		⌐	
402	★		
301	■	⌐	
632		⌐	
762	☐		
415	▨		
317		⌐	●
310	■	⌐	●

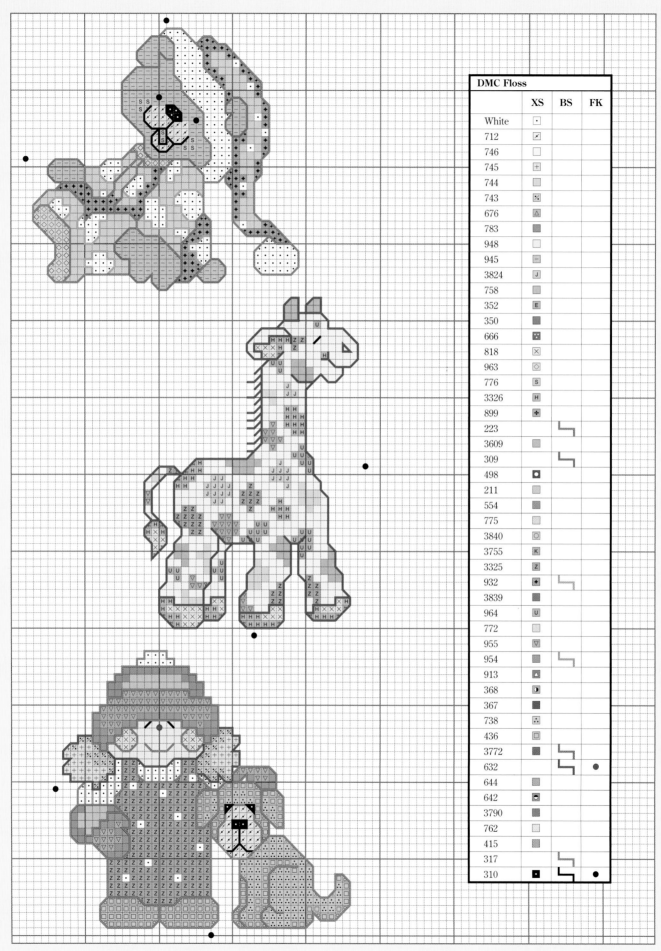

DMC Floss			
	XS	BS	FK
White	·		
712	◿		
746	▫		
745	+		
744	▪		
743	▨		
676	△		
783	◼		
948	▫		
945	⊟		
3824	J		
758	▪		
352	E		
350	◼		
666	▨		
818	⊠		
963	◇		
776	S		
3326	H		
899	✚		
223		⌐	
3609	▪		
309		⌐	
498	◻		
211	▪		
554	◼		
775	▫		
3840	◎		
3755	K		
3325	Z		
932	✚	⌐	
3839	◼		
964	U		
772	▫		
955	▽		
954	◼	⌐	
913	▲		
368	◑		
367	◼		
738	▫		
436	▢		
3772	▨	⌐	
632		⌐	●
644	▪		
642	▪		
3790	◼		
762	▫		
415	▨		
317		⌐	
310	◼	⌐	●

Bless the Animals Sampler

DMC Floss	XS	BS	FK
White	·		
745			
3821			
677	+		
676			
3825	U		
741			
776			
899	O		
351			
666	E		
304			
209			
800			
813			
826			
3348			
703	Z		
989			
987			
986		⌐	
561		⌐	
3856	−		
402	K		
3776			
301	△		
739			
738			
437	S		
436	N		
435			
434		⌐	
950	◇		
3773			
3064	G		
3772			
632	★	⌐	●
842	J		
841			
840			
3790		⌐	
3024	▽		
646			
762			
415			
318			
413		⌐	
310	▪	⌐	●

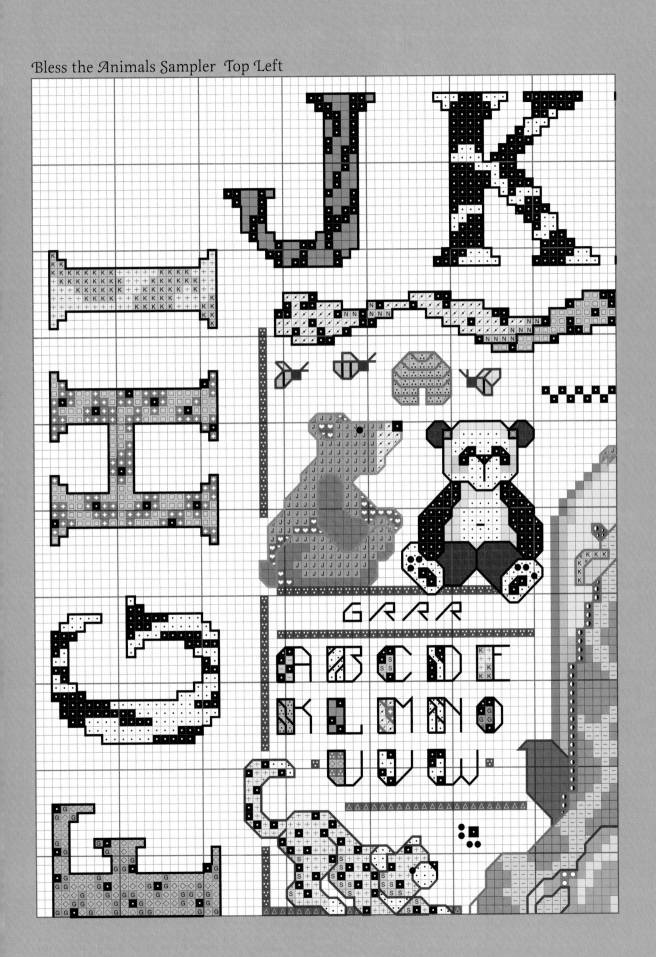

GRRR

meow

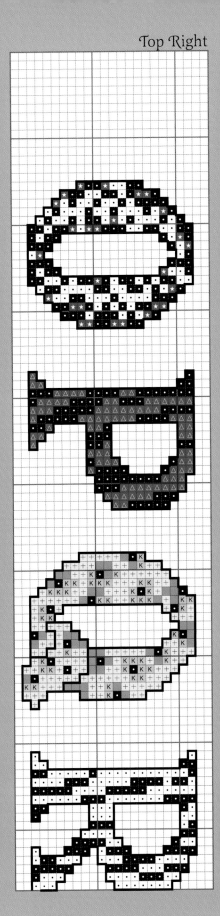

DMC Floss			DMC Floss			
	XS	BS		XS	BS	FK
White	·		3776	▪		
745	☐		301	△		
3821	▦		739	◢		
677	+		738	☐		
676	∴		437	S		
3825	U		436	N		
741	✚		435	✦		
776	☐		434	◖	⌐	
899	○		950	◇		
351	▪		3773	▪		
666	E		3064	G		
304	■		3772	▦		
209	▪		632	★	⌐	●
800	☐		842	J		
813	▣		841	▦		
826	▪		840	♥		
3348	☐		3790		⌐	
703	z		3024	▽		
989	▦		646	✳		
987	■		762	☐		
986		⌐	415	▦		
561	▣	⌐	318	◘		
3856	−		413	■	⌐	
402	K		310	▪	⌐	●

abcde
klmno
vwx

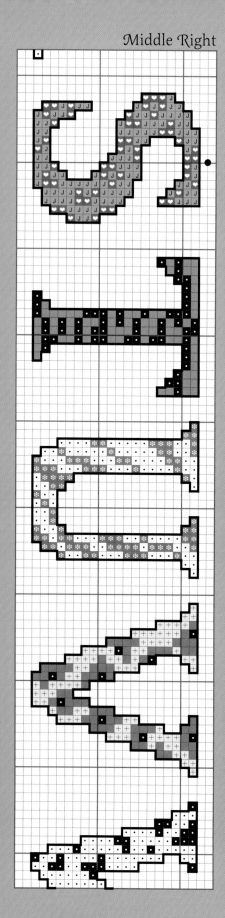

DMC Floss			DMC Floss			
	XS	BS		XS	BS	FK
White	·		3776	▣		
745	▢		301	▲		
3821	▢		739	◪		
677	+		738	▫		
676	∴		437	S		
3825	U		436	N		
741	+		435	◪		
776	▢		434	◪	⌐	
899	○		950	◇		
351	▣		3773	▣		
666	E		3064	G		
304	■		3772	▨		
209	▣		632	✦	⌐	●
800	▢		842	J		
813	◙		841	▣		
826	▣		840	♥		
3348	▢		3790		⌐	
703	Z		3024	▽		
989	▨		646	✻		
987	▣		762	▢		
986		⌐	415	▣		
561	▨	⌐	318	○		
3856	−		413	■	⌐	
402	K		310	▪	⌐	●

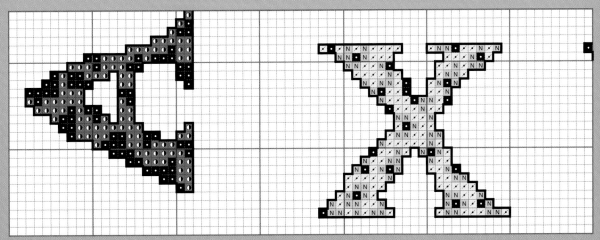

Bottom Left

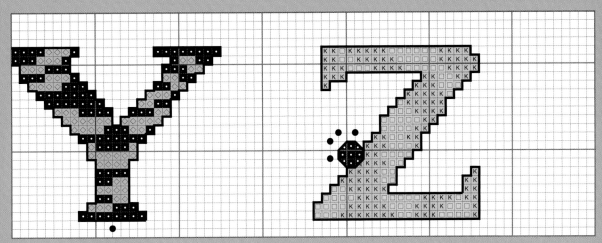

Bottom Middle

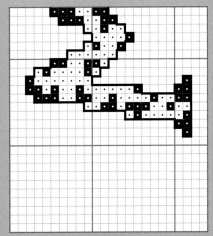

Bottom Right

My Very Best Friend

DMC Floss			
	XS	**BS**	**FK**
White	·		
Ecru	×		
3823			
744			
743	⅔		
742			
676	U		
729			
783	◑		
948			
951	–		
945			
352	⊡		
350			
963	◿		
3716			
776	△		
899	E		
3831		⌐	
3609	H		
3607	■		
800			
809	Z		
826		⌐	●
813	◓		
793	◪		
792		⌐	●
747			
3761	⣶		
964	◎		
3766	K		
369	▢		
368	★		
772			
704			
3816			
739	◇		
738	S		
3827	J		
402	W		
950	F		
407	✦		
3772	▽		
632		⌐	
3826	♥		
975		⌐	
301	■		
415			
318	N		
317	◕		
413	■	⌐	●
310	▪	⌐	

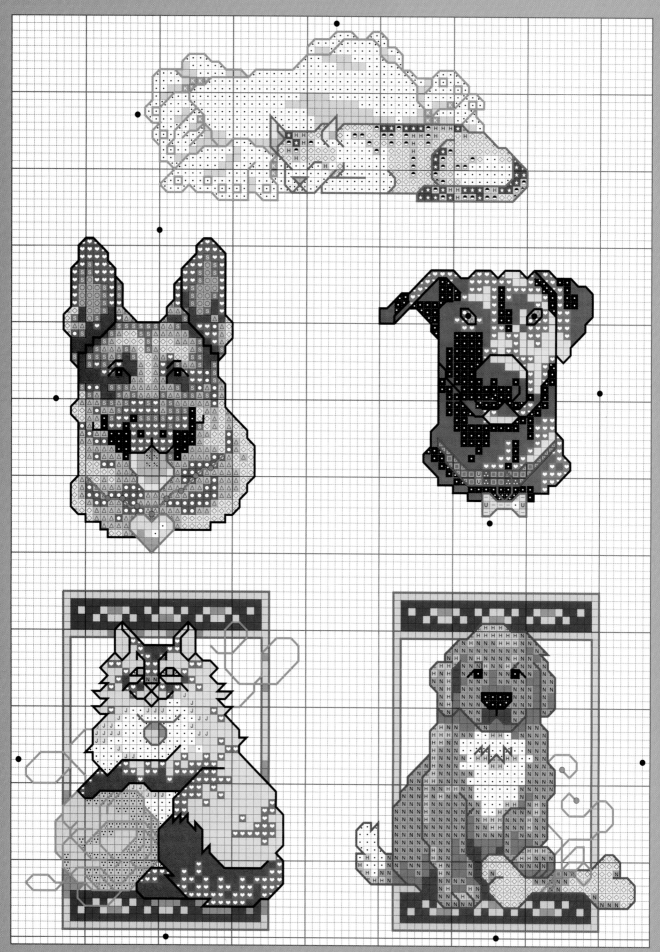

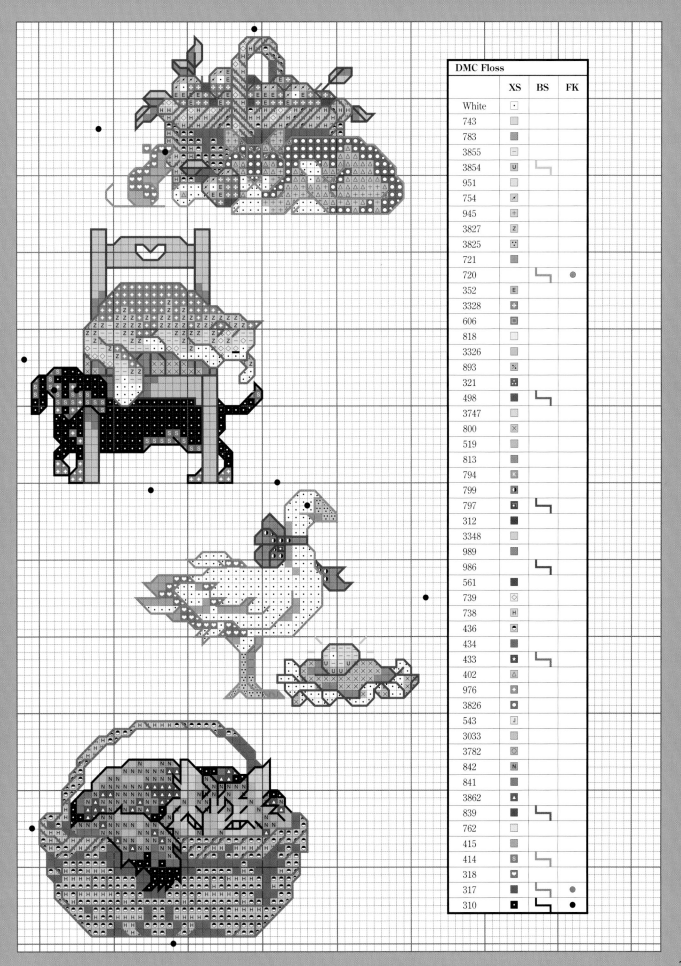

DMC Floss	XS	BS	FK
White	·		
743			
783			
3855	–		
3854	U	⌐	
951			
754			
945	+		
3827	Z		
3825	∴		
721			
720		⌐	●
352	E		
3328	✚		
606	▢		
818			
3326			
893	∷		
321	▪		
498		⌐	
3747			
800	✕		
519			
813			
794	K		
799	◑		
797	◪	⌐	
312			
3348			
989			
986		⌐	
561			
739	◇		
738	H		
436	◖		
434			
433	★	⌐	
402	△		
976	✦		
3826	◙		
543	J		
3033			
3782	O		
842	N		
841			
3862	▲		
839		⌐	
762			
415			
414	S	⌐	
318	♥		
317		⌐	●
310	▪	⌐	●

DMC Floss			
	XS	BS	FK
White	·		
746	□		
445	◹		
727	▨		
3856	J		
3855	−		
3854	▨		
945	▨		
3824	U		
722	⊙		
353	E		
606	▨		
818	▨		
3713	+		
3716	△		
961	▨		
304	■	⌐	
3753	▨		
704	▨		
504 } 369	▨		
3363	◖		
3362		⌐	
3053	▨		
3348	▽		
3347	H		
989	✚		
987	◘		
986		⌐	
3776	▣		
3826		∟	
975	▨		
543	Z		
3864	▨		
842 } 841	◲		
841	▨		
840	▨		
3862	★		
838	■	⌐	
762	▨		
415	▣		
318	K		
317	▨	⌐	●
310	■	⌐	●

Bless Our Barnyard

115

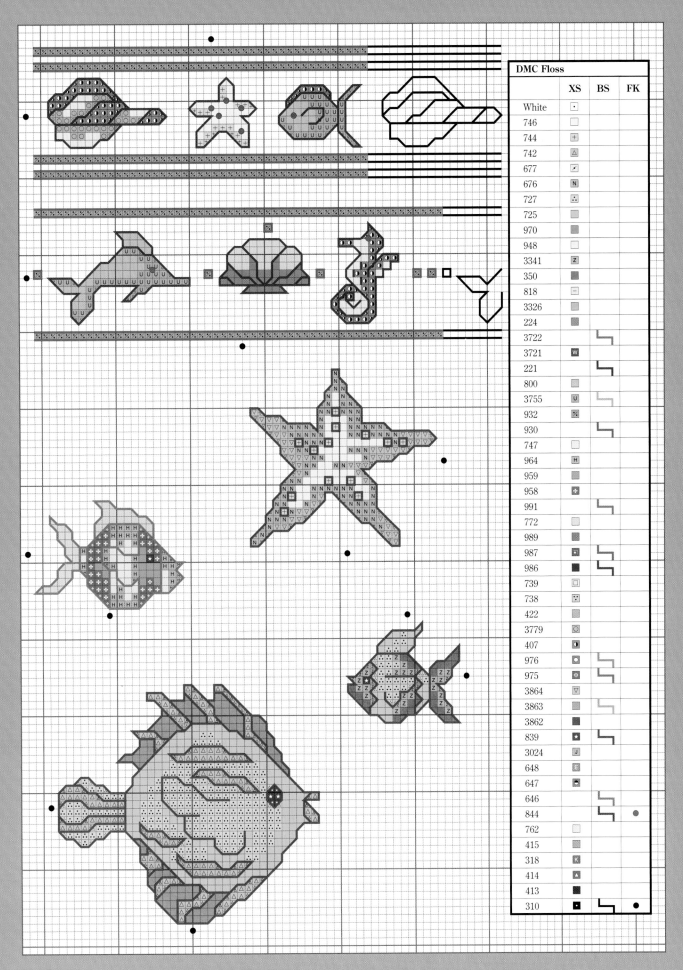

DMC Floss			
	XS	**BS**	**FK**
White	·		
746	□		
744	+		
742	△		
677	◪		
676	N		
727	⦂		
725	▨		
970	▨		
948	□		
3341	Z		
350	▨		
818	–		
3326	▨		
224	▨		
3722		⌐	
3721	W		
221		⌐	
800	▨		
3755	U	⌐	
932	⊠		
930		⌐	
747	□		
964	H		
959	▨		
958	✦		
991		⌐	
772	▨		
989	▨		
987	▣	⌐	
986	■	⌐	
739	□		
738	⦂		
422	▨		
3779	◎		
407	◑		
976	◉	⌐	
975	✳		
3864	▽		
3863	▨	⌐	
3862	▨		
839	★	⌐	
3024	J		
648	E		
647	◖		
646		⌐	
844		⌐	●
762	□		
415	▨		
318	K		
414	▲		
413	■		
310	■	⌐	●

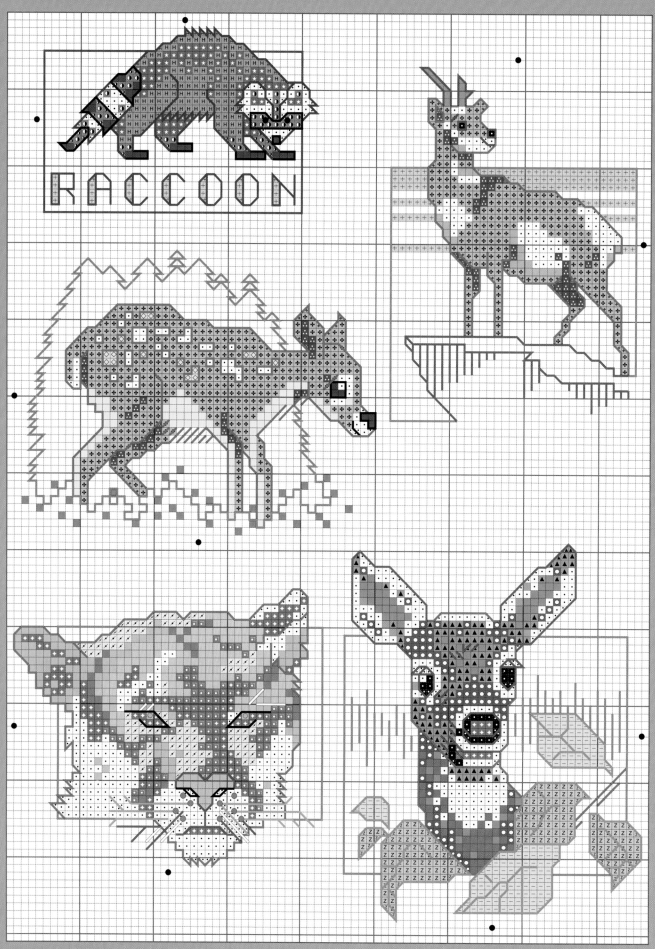

RACCOON

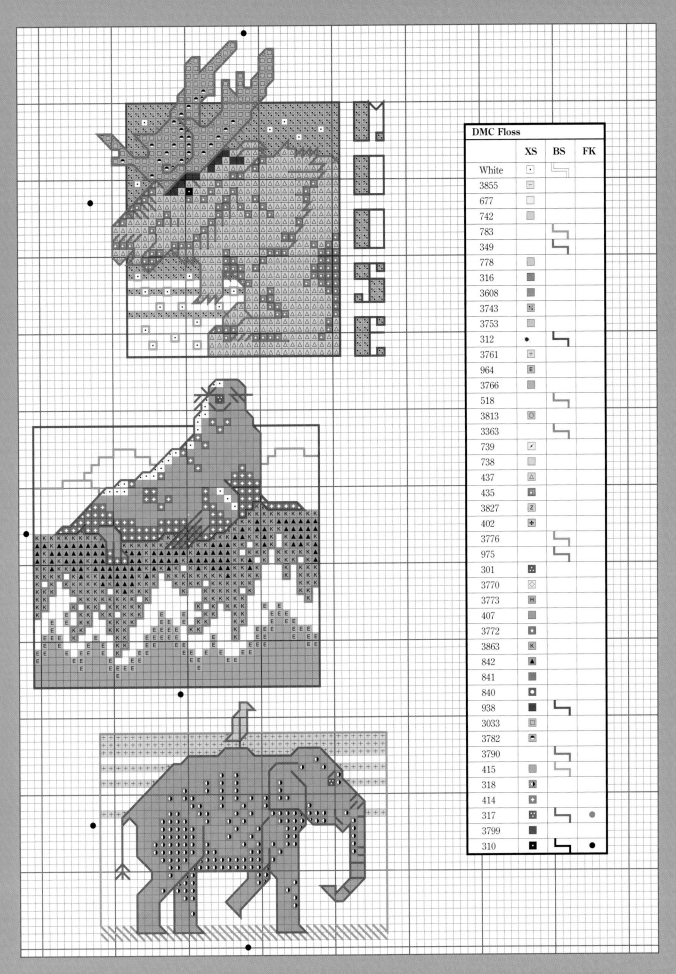

DMC Floss			
	XS	**BS**	**FK**
White	·		
3855	⊟		
677	☐		
742	▨		
783			
349			
778	▨		
316	▨		
3608	▨		
3743	▨		
3753	▨		
312	•		
3761	+		
964	E		
3766	▨		
518			
3813	◉		
3363			
739	◪		
738	▨		
437	△		
435	▣		
3827	z		
402	✚		
3776			
975			
301	▦		
3770	◇		
3773	H		
407	▨		
3772	✷		
3863	K		
842	▲		
841	▨		
840	◪		
938	▪		
3033	▣		
3782	◲		
3790			
415	▨		
318	◑		
414	✦		
317	▦		●
3799	▪		
310	◾		●

119

WOOD DUCK

DMC Floss			
	XS	BS	FK
White	·		
3855	⊠		
744			
743	△		
742			
677	⊟		
676	H		
970			
350			
963			
309			
816	■		
815			
3761			
519			
827	○		
813			
826	■		
825			
772			
703	◐		
912	■		
562			
561			
3813			
503			
3816	E		
3815	⊡		
3818	■		
739	+		
437	Z		
435	■		
434			
3773			
3778	✦		
3776	▨		
842	⊠		
840	★		
839			
415			
318	U		
414	▣		
317	▨		
413	■		●
310	■		

DMC Floss			
	XS	BS	FK
White	·		
712	▢		
3078	▢		
3855	◪		
744	▢		
742	△		
741		⌐	●
948	✕		
761	+		
776	U		
899	▢		
605	▢		
3722	▣	⌐	●
350	▣	⌐	●
349	▣		
3350		⌐	
553		⌐	●
3753	▢		
3761	▬		
775	▢		
3755		⌐	
3766	◖		
826	▣		
825		⌐	
807		⌐	
772	▢		
703	▣	⌐	
954	✦		
912	△		
561		⌐	
739	▢		
3827	◎		
976	▣	⌐	
435	z		
3826	★		
975	▣	⌐	
762	▢		
415	▣		
318	▣	⌐	
317	◙		
413	■	⌐	●

123

DMC Floss		
	XS	BS
White	·	
712		
727		
725		
3855	◪	
743	⊡	
742	✚	
741	◑	
971		
720		
608	△	
353	⊞	
349		⌐
963		
335	E	⌐
800		
3752	◓	
932		⌐
931		⌐
964	◎	
958		⌐
772		
703		⌐
3348	⊠	
3347		
913	▣	
564	▢	
562		
561		⌐
3827	J	
977	Z	
976	⊡	
3826	★	
975		⌐
739	✕	
738	H	
543	⊟	
3864		
842	✦	
841		
840	K	
839		⌐
453	▽	
3024	N	
3023		⌐
415		
318	U	
414	◎	⌐
413	✾	⌐

Anchor Conversion Chart

DMC	Anchor	DMC	Anchor	DMC	Anchor	DMC	Anchor	DMC	Anchor
B5200	1	371	887	580	924	734	279	824	164
White	2	372	887	581	281	738	361	825	162
Ecru	387	400	351	597	1064	739	366	826	161
208	110	402	1047	598	1062	740	316	827	160
209	109	407	914	600	59	741	304	828	9159
210	108	413	236	601	63	742	303	829	906
211	342	414	235	602	57	743	302	830	277
221	897	415	398	603	62	744	301	831	277
223	895	420	374	604	55	745	300	832	907
224	893	422	372	605	1094	746	275	833	874
225	1026	433	358	606	334	747	158	834	874
300	352	434	310	608	330	754	1012	838	1088
301	1049	435	365	610	889	758	9575	839	1086
304	19	436	363	611	898	760	1022	840	1084
307	289	437	362	612	832	761	1021	841	1082
309	42	444	291	613	831	762	234	842	1080
310	403	445	288	632	936	772	259	844	1041
311	148	451	233	640	393	775	128	869	375
312	979	452	232	642	392	776	24	890	218
315	1019	453	231	644	391	778	968	891	35
316	1017	469	267	645	273	780	309	892	33
317	400	470	266	646	8581	781	308	893	27
318	235	471	265	647	1040	782	308	894	26
319	1044	472	253	648	900	783	307	895	1044
320	215	498	1005	666	46	791	178	898	380
321	47	500	683	676	891	792	941	899	38
322	978	501	878	677	361	793	176	900	333
326	59	502	877	680	901	794	175	902	897
327	101	503	876	699	923	796	133	904	258
333	119	504	206	700	228	797	132	905	257
334	977	517	162	701	227	798	146	906	256
335	40	518	1039	702	226	799	145	907	255
336	150	519	1038	703	238	800	144	909	923
340	118	520	862	704	256	801	359	910	230
341	117	522	860	712	926	806	169	911	205
347	1025	523	859	718	88	807	168	912	209
349	13	524	858	720	325	809	130	913	204
350	11	535	401	721	324	813	161	915	1029
351	10	543	933	722	323	814	45	917	89
352	9	550	101	725	305	815	44	918	341
353	8	552	99	726	295	816	43	919	340
355	1014	553	98	727	293	817	13	920	1004
356	1013	554	95	729	890	818	23	921	1003
367	216	561	212	730	845	819	271	922	1003
368	214	562	210	731	281	820	134	924	851
369	1043	563	208	732	281	822	390	926	850
370	888	564	206	733	280	823	152	927	849

DMC	Anchor	DMC	Anchor	DMC	Anchor	DMC	Anchor	DMC	Anchor
928	274	3021	905	3722	1027	3816	876	114	1213
930	1035	3022	8581	3726	1018	3817	875	115	1206
931	1034	3023	899	3727	1016	3818	923	121	1210
932	1033	3024	388	3731	76	3819	278	122	1215
934	862	3031	905	3733	75	3820	306	123	——
935	861	3032	898	3740	872	3821	305	124	1210
936	846	3033	387	3743	869	3822	295	125	1213
937	268	3041	871	3746	1030	3823	386	126	1209
938	381	3042	870	3747	120	3824	8		
939	152	3045	888	3750	1036	3825	323		
943	189	3046	887	3752	1032	3826	1049		
945	881	3047	852	3753	1031	3827	311		
946	332	3051	845	3755	140	3828	373		
947	330	3052	844	3756	1037	3829	901		
948	1011	3053	843	3760	162	3830	5975		
950	4146	3064	883	3761	928				
951	1010	3072	397	3765	170	**Variegated**			
954	203	3078	292	3766	167	**Colors**			
955	203	3325	129	3768	779				
956	40	3326	36	3770	1009	48	1207		
957	50	3328	1024	3772	1007	51	1220		
958	187	3340	329	3773	1008	52	1209		
959	186	3341	328	3774	778	53	——		
961	76	3345	268	3776	1048	57	1203		
962	75	3346	267	3777	1015	61	1218		
963	23	3347	266	3778	1013	62	1201		
964	185	3348	264	3779	868	67	1212		
966	240	3350	77	3781	1050	69	1218		
970	925	3354	74	3782	388	75	1206		
971	316	3362	263	3787	904	90	1217		
972	298	3363	262	3790	904	91	1211		
973	290	3364	261	3799	236	92	1215		
975	357	3371	382	3801	1098	93	1210		
976	1001	3607	87	3802	1019	94	1216		
977	1002	3608	86	3803	69	95	1209		
986	246	3609	85	3804	63	99	1204		
987	244	3685	1028	3805	62	101	1213		
988	243	3687	68	3806	62	102	1209		
989	242	3688	75	3807	122	103	1210		
991	1076	3689	49	3808	1068	104	1217		
992	1072	3705	35	3809	1066	105	1218		
993	1070	3706	33	3810	1066	106	1203		
995	410	3708	31	3811	1060	107	1203		
996	433	3712	1023	3812	188	108	1220		
3011	856	3713	1020	3813	875	111	1218		
3012	855	3716	25	3814	1074	112	1201		
3013	853	3721	896	3815	877	113	1210		

Metric Equivalancy Chart

mm-millimetres cm-centimetres
inches to millimetres and centimetres

inches	mm	cm	inches	cm	inches	cm
1/8	3	0.3	9	22.9	30	76.2
1/4	6	0.6	10	25.4	31	78.7
3/8	10	1.0	11	27.9	32	81.3
1/2	13	1.3	12	30.5	33	83.8
5/8	16	1.6	13	33.0	34	86.4
3/4	19	1.9	14	35.6	35	88.9
7/8	22	2.2	15	38.1	36	91.4
1	25	2.5	16	40.6	37	94.0
1 1/4	32	3.2	17	43.2	38	96.5
1 1/2	38	3.8	18	45.7	39	99.1
1 3/4	44	4.4	19	48.3	40	101.6
2	51	5.1	20	50.8	41	104.1
2 1/2	64	6.4	21	53.3	42	106.7
3	76	7.6	22	55.9	43	109.2
3 1/2	89	8.9	23	58.4	44	111.8
4	102	10.2	24	61.0	45	114.3
4 1/2	114	11.4	25	63.5	46	116.8
5	127	12.7	26	66.0	47	119.4
6	152	15.2	27	68.6	48	121.9
7	178	17.8	28	71.1	49	124.5
8	203	20.3	29	73.7	50	127.0

Index